Lee Canter's
CLASSROOM
Management
for *Academic Success*

Solution Tree

Copyright © 2006 by Solution Tree
(formerly National Educational Service)
555 North Morton Street
Bloomington, IN 47404
(800) 733-6786 (toll free) / (812) 336-7700
Fax: (812) 336-7790
email: info@solution-tree.com
www.solution-tree.com

Cover and CD Design by Grannan Graphic Design, Ltd.
Text Design and Composition by TG Design Group

Printed in the United States of America
ISBN 978-1-932127-83-6

Dedication

To Leticia Rodriguez

Your dedication to making a difference in the lives of
underserved children is an inspiration to me!

Table of Contents

Acknowledgements

As with any book I have written over my career, this book would not have seen the light of day without the assistance of many dedicated, supportive, and talented individuals.

To Jeff Jones, president of Solution Tree, thank you for believing in the value of my efforts to assist educators. This book would not exist without your support.

To Rhonda Rieseberg, your input and feedback were invaluable to shaping this book. I am deeply appreciative to you for all your efforts, and I look forward to working with you again soon on my next project.

To Barbara, not only did you edit the manuscript, but you continue to light up my life!

Finally, to all the teachers I have had the honor to work with over the years, your dedication to our nation's youth drives my efforts each day.

About the Author

Lee Canter is the internationally recognized author of over 40 best-selling books for educators and the developer of acclaimed educational training programs, including *Assertive Discipline*®, *Succeeding With Difficult Students*®, and *Parents on Your Side*®. The Assertive Discipline program has been the gold standard in the field since it was first published in 1976.

Known as one of the most dynamic speakers and trainers in education today, Canter has keynoted countless conferences and has been a frequent guest on noted television programs, including *The Oprah Winfrey Show, The Today Show,* and *Good Morning America.* He and his staff have trained over 1.5 million teachers.

Introduction

In 1997 I sold my company, Canter and Associates, to Sylvan Learning Systems, Inc. Finally, after flying more than one million miles and training more than one million teachers all over the world, I felt it was time to retire. I moved to quaint and scenic Carmel-by-the-Sea, California, to finally take life easy.

I wasn't long into my retirement when I started to receive requests from educators for help. The message was almost always the same:

> *"We're under enormous pressure to raise academic achievement, but our efforts are constantly stymied by a small group of students whose disruptive behavior impacts the entire learning environment of the classroom."*

These educators needed a comprehensive, easy-to-use resource with a step-by-step approach for creating a classroom environment that would promote academic success for all students. *Classroom Management for Academic Success* was written to meet this need. In writing this book, I took three distinct steps to make it comprehensive and practical.

First, I thoroughly reviewed the latest and best books in the field of classroom management. It was vital that the concepts and strategies presented to teachers were, whenever possible, validated as being effective by educational researchers.

Second, I observed and interviewed selected master teachers—teachers who have been recognized by their peers as professionals who can effectively motivate their students. From these master teachers, I collected the ideas and techniques that they believe are critical to their classroom management success.

Finally, I took note when teachers told me that concepts and strategies in my previous works made a difference in how they managed student behavior. I have included and further developed these concepts in *Classroom Management for Academic Success*. In particular, I have expanded the concepts in the three editions of *Assertive Discipline: Positive Behavior*

Management for Today's Classroom and in *Lee Canter's Responsible Behavior Curriculum Guide.*

From *Assertive Discipline,* I build on the basic concepts of how a teacher's expectations impact his or her ability to motivate students to be successful. In addition, I elaborate on the strategies needed to teach students responsible behavior through the use of a classroom management plan.

From the *Responsible Behavior Curriculum Guide,* I adapt the concept of developing a curriculum unit on responsible behavior that is taught at the beginning of the school year. I also expand the concepts and strategies on how to effectively manage behavior in the countless activities of a school day.

So, my retirement was short-lived! I quickly realized I missed the honor and privilege of working with so many talented teachers. For those who have encountered problems in classroom management, I am grateful for the opportunity to write *Classroom Management for Academic Success* to help you bring out the best in every one of your students.

Part 1

Overview of Classroom Management for Academic Success

Chapter 1

Classroom Management: The Key to Improving Academic Performance

"How can I raise student test scores when I spend so much time just trying to get the students to listen to me and follow my directions?"

"I can't get through the new curriculum because my students are too disruptive and inattentive."

"Often the behavior of some students is so disruptive that learning stops in the classroom."

Do any of the statements above sound familiar? If so, you are not alone. In an era when improving academic achievement is the number one priority for most teachers, many educators are shackled in their efforts by their inability to effectively manage the disruptive behavior of one or more students.

Consider the following statistics:

- Seventy-seven percent of teachers admit that their teaching would be more effective if they did not have to spend so much time dealing with disruptive students (Public Agenda, 2004).

- Forty percent of teachers spend more time keeping order than teaching (Johnson, 2004).

- Fifty percent of teacher time is spent dealing with disruptive behavior in many classrooms in America and at all grade levels (Cotton, 1990; Walker, Colvin, & Ramsey, 1995).

THE IMPORTANCE OF CLASSROOM MANAGEMENT SKILLS

In the last few years, research has clearly confirmed what we have long suspected: A teacher's skill level is a critical factor in improving the academic achievement of his or her students (Good and Brophy, 2003; Marzano, Marzano, & Pickering, 2003). As a result, great effort has been made toward improving the classroom skills of today's teachers. The greater part of these efforts has focused on providing teachers with more effective instructional strategies and standards-based curriculum to facilitate student learning.

As important as it is to improve your ability to use more effective instructional strategies and standards-based curriculum, one factor is significantly more critical to your ability to improve student performance:

> The key to raising student achievement is your ability to effectively manage student behavior (Wright, Horn, & Sanders, 1997; Wang, Haertel, & Walberg, 1993).
>
> No instructional strategy will be effective if you are unable to get all students to quickly follow your directions to get and stay on task.
>
> No matter how sophisticated your curriculum is, you will never successfully implement it until you can get your students on task and engaged.

How much can effective classroom management impact achievement? In *Classroom Management That Works: Research-Based Strategies for Every Teacher,* noted researcher Robert Marzano found that:

> Teachers who master effective classroom management skills can raise the achievement of their students by a dramatic 20 percentile points.

TEACHERS DO NOT RECEIVE EFFECTIVE CLASSROOM MANAGEMENT TRAINING

Why do so many teachers have a difficult time creating a calm, orderly classroom environment that promotes academic success? An observation I made more than 25 years ago rings true today:

> Teachers are not trained how to motivate *all* of their students to behave successfully in the classroom.

Most teachers are trained in classroom management programs that research suggests work with "compliant" students. Basically, compliant students are those who want to please you. They respond quickly to your positive actions, discipline, or both. Typically, compliant students make up approximately 80-90% of most classrooms (Curwin & Mendler, 1999; Sugai, Horner, & Gresham, 2002).

What about the remaining 10-20%? These are students who, for countless reasons, are noncompliant.

> Noncompliant students are much more interested in doing what they want, when and how they want, rather than in pleasing you.

Your basic approaches to motivate noncompliant students to choose to behave are simply not effective with them. Not being trained to successfully motivate these students to behave

> How many disruptive, noncompliant students does it take to lower the academic achievement of an entire class? You know the answer: only one!

appropriately has an enormous detrimental impact on any classroom. Consider this question:

You are not alone in knowing it only takes one disruptive student to monopolize your time and impact the academic climate—*your students know this as well* (Walker, Ramsey, & Gresham, 2004). A recent study shows that more than 40% of students believe that the behavior of another student had hindered their academic performance (Gordon, 1999).

YOU CAN LEARN TO BE AN EFFECTIVE CLASSROOM MANAGER

If you are struggling with classroom management issues that negatively impact student learning and achievement, your situation is not hopeless. There are solutions to your problems.

On a regular basis, my staff and I work with teachers of all grade levels and in schools of every socioeconomic condition who have learned how to motivate *all* of their students—even the ones considered noncompliant by colleagues—to behave successfully in their classrooms.

Why are these teachers able to motivate their students to behave appropriately in the classroom when their peers have been unsuccessful? Are they simply "naturals" who were born to teach challenging students?

Yes, a small percentage of these teachers are uniquely gifted educators, but the vast majority of teachers are simply ordinary educators who learn specific "attributes" for dealing with students. These attributes enable these teachers to succeed with noncompliant students who continue to challenge their colleagues.

Most importantly, research and experience clearly indicate any teacher who is motivated has the potential to learn the characteristics of successful colleagues and dramatically reduce the disruptive behavior in his or her classroom (Emmer, Sanford, Clements, & Martin, 1982; Marzano, Marzano, & Pickering, 2003). Each year we work with thousands of educators who use the insights they gain from studying effective classroom managers to transform how they deal with students, reduce their frustration, and finally get their students to be more successful than they ever thought possible.

CHARACTERISTICS OF EFFECTIVE CLASSROOM MANAGERS

What is the difference between effective classroom managers and their peers? Based on the years I have spent studying this question, the answer is clear. Teachers who create a classroom environment that promotes academic success have the following attributes:

They Have Empowering Beliefs

These teachers believe they are capable of influencing *all* students to behave in a positive manner—even those considered to be noncompliant.

They Teach Policies and Procedures at the Beginning of the School Year

The number one priority for these teachers is to systematically teach all students appropriate behavior for all classroom activities. This establishes an environment that promotes academic success.

They Motivate All Students to Quickly Follow Directions and to Get and Stay on Task

Effective teachers use research-validated management strategies designed to motivate all students to quickly follow directions and get on task. These strategies include the following:

1. Clearly communicate expectations for how students are to successfully behave throughout the day or period.

2. Provide positive feedback to students who meet the expectations.

3. Take corrective action with students who do not meet the expectations.

They Build Trusting Relationships With All of Their Students

These teachers recognize that students need to believe the teacher has their best interest at heart before they will choose to behave. The teachers therefore use best practices to build positive relationships with each student.

They Use Effective Instructional Strategies

These teachers recognize that a key to effective management is to keep the students actively engaged in the learning process. To do so, they use research-validated engagement strategies in their teaching.

They Plan How to Effectively Manage Student Behavior in All Classroom Activities

In addition to planning how to conduct instruction, these teachers also consistently plan how they will manage student behavior during all classroom activities (for example, during instruction and transitions).

YOU CAN DO IT!

You, too, can transform how you deal with your students. You can establish a classroom environment that promotes academic success for all of your students. As so many of your colleagues have done, you can master the attributes of effective classroom managers.

All it takes is a commitment on your part to be open to the possibility that there are different, more effective ways to view student behavior, why they do what they do, how you relate and respond to your students, and the potential influence you absolutely do have to motivate them to choose to succeed in your classroom.

I invite you to be open and reexamine what you do and why you do it when it comes to classroom management. Consider the possibility that rather than feeling frustrated, you have the opportunity to feel success as you create a classroom environment where you can teach and students can learn free from the distraction of disruptive behavior!

Part 2

Empowering Beliefs and Expectations

Chapter 2

I Can Transform My Classroom Management Efforts

Transforming your classroom management efforts begins with a close look at your expectations and beliefs. Why? The foundation of your ability to create a classroom environment that promotes academic success rests on your beliefs and expectations regarding your ability to influence student behavior.

In order to be an effective classroom manager, you need to have a high degree of *efficacy*—in other words, you must believe you can make a difference with all of your students (Emmer & Hickman, 1991; Walker, Ramsey, & Gresham, 2004).

The core expectations and beliefs of effective teachers are reflected in the following expectations and beliefs:

- *"All of my students can behave appropriately."*

- *"I can influence all of my students to choose to behave appropriately."*

- *"It is okay to expect and demand all of my students to behave appropriately."*

The reality is that the vast majority of teachers who struggle with classroom management issues have unreasonably low expectations regarding their ability to influence the behavior of their noncompliant "problem" students (Canter & Canter, 1992). These teachers typically undermine their own efforts by having the following disempowering expectations and beliefs:

- *"Some students have so many problems—emotional, behavioral, familial, and socioeconomic—that they cannot control their behavior."*

- *"Because of student problems, I am unable to influence them to behave appropriately."*

- *"It can be harmful to the students to expect and demand that they behave appropriately."*

You have probably heard the axiom: "If you think you can or can't, you're right." As tired as most of us are of hearing this, there is much truth in the message. If you believe you *can* influence students to behave successfully in your classroom, there will be a dramatically higher probability that you will get positive results from the management strategies you use. On the other hand, if you believe for any reason that you *cannot* influence students, your chance of success is equally diminished no matter what management approach you try to use.

Instead of an esoteric discussion on the effect that teacher expectations and beliefs have on their ability to influence students, I offer a dramatic example of the power of beliefs and expectations that clearly illustrates the point.

A number of years ago, I was brought in to train the staff of a school with a reputation for having the worst discipline problems in the district. The school's issues were so bad that the district had put it on their "under-performing" school list and was seriously considering reassigning the administration and most of the teachers and bringing in an intervention team to run the school.

The school was located in the lowest socioeconomic area of the district, with more than 90% of the students on the free lunch program. The teachers reported that many students were so troubled and had so many overwhelming problems that the teachers believed there was no way to motivate the students to behave in the classroom. In addition, many teachers were new to the profession and simply did not feel capable of getting those "troubled, problem students" to listen to them.

After I conducted a training session at the school, the teachers returned to their classrooms and tried to apply the strategies they had learned. Though they had success with some students, a core group of noncompliant students remained out of control. These students would shout, run around the rooms, and openly defy their teachers.

I was contacted again and given the grim update on many of the problems the teachers faced. I agreed to return to the school to offer additional assistance. As I typically do under these circumstances, I arranged to spend several hours observing in classrooms to get a firsthand look at the problems before I worked again with the teachers.

Considering what I had been told, I expected the worst and entered the building with much trepidation. However, I was surprised by what I saw. In the first classroom I entered, I observed students quietly following the teacher's directions and quickly getting and staying on task. Going from classroom to classroom, I saw again and again calm, positive environments where teachers were teaching and students were learning, free of disruptive behavior.

Feeling slightly bewildered, I met with the school's staff later in the day. I began the session by explaining that, given what I had been told, I was surprised at the lack of problems I had observed in the classrooms.

To my chagrin, a teacher immediately spoke up and said, "You have not seen an accurate picture of how bad the discipline problems really are. Today was far from a typical day since the district's evaluation team was in the school again." The principal then quickly apologized for having me come and observe on this day, since he had forgotten it coincided with the return visit of the evaluation team.

Confused by what I had just been told, I asked why my visit on that particular day was such an issue. Another teacher quickly said, "You don't realize the importance of this visit. Our previous review was extremely negative and a major issue was the lack of discipline in the classrooms. One more poor report and the district may bring a team in to intervene in the running of this school."

Other teachers spoke up, and their comments were summarized by one teacher who stated, "We all met and decided we had to lay it on the line with the students. We told them that the state accreditation team was going to be here today and the future of the school depended upon receiving a positive report. Thus, we all let the students know there was no way we were going to tolerate any misbehavior. Without exception, every student was expected to do what he or she was told to do during class without any talking out, disrupting, arguing, or fighting. The bottom line is we let the students know that we meant business."

As I listened to these comments, the proverbial lightbulb came on in my head! Here we had the *same* teachers dealing with the *same* students with the *same* problems using the *same* classroom management approach, yet the students behaved in a totally different manner from one day to the next. What had changed? Nothing but the teachers' expectations.

During the district evaluation team visit, these teachers believed it was critical that all students behave appropriately, including those students with "problems." Therefore, the teachers thought it was okay to expect and insist that students act appropriately. The teachers basically "raised the bar" for the type of behavior they expected. Lo and behold, the students chose to behave! What became crystal clear to me was this:

> **If teachers can motivate the students to behave successfully on one day, they have the ability to do so on any other day!**

Though the future of your school may not be on the line, something just as important or more so is. Your future success and the success of your students is on the line until you get in touch with the positive influence you really do have to motivate all of your students.

In the following chapters we will focus on why you and so many other teachers might have negative expectations and disempowering beliefs regarding your ability to influence the behavior of many of your students. Then we will examine how you can promote a positive academic atmosphere in your classroom by raising your expectations, developing a high level of efficacy, and establishing a mind set that dramatically increases your ability to motivate your students to engage in appropriate behavior.

Chapter 3

My Students Can Behave Appropriately

You cannot have high expectations of your ability to influence students unless you sincerely believe students can control their behavior and do what is asked of them. Unfortunately, all too many teachers believe that some students have such serious problems that they cannot behave like their peers, no matter what classroom management strategies are used (Canter & Canter, 1992).

In reality, you do have students who have significant problems. That is not the issue. Here is the issue:

> Do the problems your students have really prevent them from being able to control their behavior and to do what you want them to?

PROBLEM CATEGORIES

I suggest that if you objectively examine the actual impact most student problems have on their ability to control their behavior, you will be surprised by what you will find. To help you examine these issues, I have identified a number of problems that educators believe can so adversely affect students as to keep them from behaving appropriately in school. As you read each category, think about students you have had, or now have, in relation to the questions on how their problems actually affect their behavior.

Emotional or Psychological Problems

"Carla is so angry and defiant. She needs intensive therapy to get her temper under control so she can behave in the classroom."

One of the most common beliefs—you could say a "scared cow" of educational psychology—is the perception that inappropriate student behavior is the result of deep-seated emotional or psychological problems.

Obviously, some of your students have emotional issues that can profoundly affect their self-concept, attitudes, and responses. They may have experienced emotional neglect, trauma, or both. As serious as the impact of these experiences are on students, the question continues to be: Do these "emotional problems" prevent the student from being able to function appropriately in the classroom? Think about this as you ask yourself the following questions:

- How do the emotional problems of my students prevent them from doing what I want them to do?

- Why do the problems they have only cause them to engage in certain behaviors such as shouting out and having tantrums rather than other behaviors like fighting and stealing?

- Why do some students with emotional problems behave well in class?

Inadequate Parenting

"Adam's father is gone, and his mother can't handle him. He runs the household, and it is understandable that he is not going to listen to his teacher."

The vast majority of educators believe that many student behavior problems can be directly traced to dysfunctional home environments and the inadequate parenting that the students received.

You may have students who come from home environments that have serious detrimental effects on their development, their attitude toward school, or both. Although this is true, the issue we have to examine is the impact that inadequate parenting has on these students' ability to do what you want them to do in the classroom. Ask yourself:

- What proof do I have that those students who have received inadequate parenting are actually prevented from being able to do what I want them to do in the classroom?

- Why do some students from homes with the most dysfunctional parents have no problems at all in the classroom?

- Why do some students from the "best" homes have serious behavior problems?

Poverty

"Andrea is from the Projects, and she has so much to deal with each day. How can I expect her to come to class and act like the other students?"

Another common belief among educators is that you cannot expect too much from students raised in difficult socioeconomic environments that include serious deprivations and often violence and crime.

Although your students may be raised in poverty and may come from drug- and gang-infested neighborhoods where they learn antisocial behavior, does being raised in a challenging environment prevent your students from doing what you want them to do? Consider the following questions:

- Why do some students from disadvantaged socioeconomic areas listen to everything I say and pose no disciplinary problems?

- Why do some students from high socioeconomic areas have behavior problems?

Special Education

"Janette has learning disabilities and has been labeled a 'special ed' student. I cannot expect her to behave in my classroom."

Most educators believe that special education students are different, and that many of them have serious problems that make it difficult for them to behave appropriately in any classroom, especially one designed for "regular education" students.

Special education students face real challenges in school. They may have learning or behavioral issues that can make it more difficult for them to be successful in the classroom, and some special education students have organic problems that affect their ability to control their behavior (see page 19 for more information). When you consider special education students, think about the following questions:

- Do all special education students have behavior problems?

- How can I explain that sometimes the special education students in my class listen to me when the regular education students do not?

- Why do some special education students behave in their special education classroom but do not behave in my class?

SYSTEMATICALLY QUESTION YOUR BELIEFS

We have begun the process of questioning your beliefs regarding the impact these problems have on your students' abilities to control their behavior. To help you explore this crucial issue, you can complete this exercise:

1. Think about the problem students you have had in your classes.

2. Think about their inappropriate or disruptive behavior.

3. Ask yourself the following questions in this section as they relate to your beliefs about your students' inability to do what you want them to do.

Did the Students Behave Appropriately at the Beginning of the School Year?

Think about the first days of the school year. Did the students do what you asked? If you are like the vast majority of teachers, your response will be yes. In fact, the name for the serene interval that occurs during the first days of school is the "honeymoon period."

Why are students so compliant at the start of the year? What about their emotional problems or difficult backgrounds? Are they in "remission" when school begins?

When students first meet you, they do not know your expectations for behavior. During this honeymoon period, they find out how strict you will be by paying attention to what you do when students do or do not follow your directions. In other words, the students will "choose" to do what you want until you have been fully assessed by them and they decide if they have to listen to you.

Would the Students Behave Appropriately if the Principal Came Into the Classroom to Observe?

Imagine what would happen if the principal sat down next to a "problem" student. Do you think the student would quickly "shape up?" Your answer is probably yes—but why? Most students immediately shape up when the principal enters the room because they do not want to get into trouble.

What happens to the student's lack of control that has resulted from "years of inadequate parenting"? Is the principal the "magic pill" for ill behavior? If the student behaves when the principal comes in, then the student is obviously in control of his or her own behavior.

Do the Students Behave Appropriately With Other Teachers?

When these students are with other teachers, do they behave appropriately? For example, maybe you sent the student to another teacher's classroom because he was so disruptive in yours, and the other teacher later told you he did exactly what was asked of him. Or perhaps you observed the student in another teacher's classroom earlier or later in the day, and his or her behavior was perfectly appropriate. How can you explain this?

Do the effects of neglect or deprivation the child has suffered at home temporarily go away? Simply put, if the student is capable of controlling behavior in one teacher's classroom, he or she is capable of doing so in your classroom as well.

Could Offering a Monetary Reward Change These Students' Behavior?

As absurd as this seems, there is a very important point to be gained by considering this question. You may be thinking, "Well, of course, if I did something as outrageous as give

The Only Exception: Students With Organic Disorders

A very small percentage of students cannot control their behavior. These students have organic conditions such as autism and schizophrenia. Students who truly have attention deficit disorder (ADD) and attention deficit/hyperactivity disorder (ADHD) may also fall into this category. I qualify this, though, since so many students who have been given the ADD or ADHD label are inaccurately diagnosed (Armstrong, 1997, Greenspan & Salomon, 1996).

In order to clearly identify those students who cannot control their behavior, consider the example of a teacher I worked with who had a student with epilepsy. In the middle of class one day, the student had a grand mal seizure, which obviously disrupted the entire class. Could the teacher in any way influence the student to stop the seizure that brought the learning in the classroom to a dramatic halt? Of course not! A child with epilepsy has no control over his or her behavior nor obviously does the teacher.

her $50, she would behave, but I can't be 'paying off' my students to get them to behave!" I agree and am not advocating you take such inappropriate action.

Here is the point of this hypothetical question: If the student would choose to behave for $50, is this student in control of his or her behavior? The answer is an obvious yes! This student is making choices every day about whether or not to comply with your expectations.

YOUR STUDENTS CAN BEHAVE!

If your students choose to behave in any of the circumstances discussed above, they are telling you *they **can** behave.* If they can control their behavior at the beginning of school or when the principal comes in the room, they are capable of controlling their behavior whenever they want.

Even though your students may have very serious problems, the reality is that the problems do not prevent them from controlling their behavior. The students **can** behave, but often they **do not want** to behave.

There is a profound difference between believing your students cannot behave versus believing they *will not* behave. If you believe a student absolutely cannot behave, what potential influence do you have to change his or her behavior? None! Why bother putting in the time and effort trying to help students change their behavior when the causes are beyond their control and, consequently, beyond your control as well?

If you believe the students cannot behave, you will naturally lower your expectations for behavior. In essence you are saying, "How can I expect them to behave like the other students?" Unfortunately, the students will sense your lowered expectations and respond accordingly—they will continue acting in inappropriate and disruptive ways (Rosenthal, 1974; Weinstein & McKowan, 1998).

If you believe a student's problems prevent him or her from being able to behave, you allow yourself to be a victim of the student's circumstances. As a result, you choose to put up with the frustration of dealing with the disruptive behavior.

> On the other hand, if you recognize the reality of your students' ability to control behavior when they want to, you are empowered to use strategies that will motivate students to choose to do what you want them to do, just like the other students in the classroom.

The first step to raising your expectations is to recognize your belief that students cannot control their behavior is basically misguided. The overwhelming majority of your students—including those you consider noncompliant—*can* control their behavior. Therefore, you have the potential to positively influence them to do so.

Chapter 4

I Can Influence My Students to Behave Appropriately

Effective classroom managers not only believe that their students can behave appropriately, but they also believe they have the ability to influence their students to choose to do so. Again, these teachers have a positive sense of personal efficacy that is critical to their success (Brophy, 1996).

At this point you may be thinking, "I recognize that students with problems can behave in school, but I honestly feel I don't have what it takes to get them to listen to me." You are disheartened with your lack of success with some students and feel it just may be your "lot in life" to have to put up with students disrupting the learning environment in your classroom.

RAISING THE BAR

These negative expectations are misguided. In reality you have much more potential influence over your students than you are aware of.

Your negative perceptions of your inability to motivate students to behave are similar to the perceptions of the teachers discussed in chapter 2 who honestly believed they could not influence their students to stop disrupting the learning environment in their classroom. But when the accreditation team visited the school, these teachers raised the bar and expected all students to behave appropriately—and the students responded accordingly.

This is a simple example of a profound empowering truth:

> When teachers raise their expectations for student behavior, student behavior responds accordingly (Rosenthal, 1974; Tauber, 1999).

To raise your expectations of your ability to influence student behavior, it is important to recognize that you are also capable of raising the bar with your students. In fact, I suspect there have been occasions when you have raised the bar and have motivated all of your students, including those you consider noncompliant, to behave successfully.

The following examples are typical occasions when most teachers raise the bar for student behavior. As you read through the examples, think about your own experiences and reflect on these questions:

- How have my students—especially those that I consider noncompliant—behaved on these occasions?

- What does their behavior on these occasions say about my true potential to positively influence student behavior?

Standardized Testing Day

Think about what happens in your classroom during the days you give high-stakes mandated achievement tests. Do the students, including those you usually consider noncompliant, behave the way you want them to while taking the test? The answer most likely is, "Of course, they do!"

> On testing day, you believe what is occurring is so important that the students must cooperate and behave appropriately. Yet isn't everything you teach important to the students? Why don't they have to behave every day?

If you can get your students, even those with "problems," to do what you want on testing days, why can't you get them to do what you want any other day?

Special Visitors in Your Classroom

You may have had a special visitor come to your classroom. Perhaps this person was a dignitary, a high-ranking school district official, or any individual for whom you wanted the students to make a good impression. How did the students behave? If your experience was typical, I would guess your students did exactly what you wanted while the visitor was in your classroom. Why?

> The reason for this exceptional behavior is your resolve to not be humiliated by any of your students acting up during the visit. As a result, you raised your expectations for student behavior, and you let your students know you were serious about their behavior.

If you can influence the students to do what you want when a visitor is present, you can influence them at other times as well.

Days You Are Ill

Remember a day when you did not feel well. You had a bad cold, the flu, laryngitis, or some other malady that made you feel awful. Maybe you did not feel well because of the stress of trying to handle your noncompliant students. How did the students behave that day? If you are like most teachers, you will respond, "They behaved just fine."

> On days when you are sick, your words and actions sent a very clear message to the students: "When I'm sick like I am today, I won't tolerate any misbehaving—no excuses!"

This is the most bizarre finding of my entire career: *On days when teachers are sick, they are usually effective classroom managers.* In my seminars, I jokingly say that the way for teachers to solve their behavior issues is to pretend to be sick the entire year!

The point again is this: If the students can behave on days you are sick, there is no reason they cannot behave any other day.

WHY ARE YOU EFFECTIVE SOME OF THE TIME?

As we have seen in the previous examples, there are times when most teachers are able to effectively influence students to behave appropriately. What do you do differently that produces the results you want and need?

You Believe It Is Okay to Raise the Bar

On these occasions you believe you are justified in raising the bar regarding the behavior you expect from your students. You are not concerned about being too firm or strict—concerns that plague many classroom management efforts (see chapter 5, page 25). Your priority becomes making sure the students simply behave appropriately—they take the test, are respectful to visitors, or do not misbehave on days when you do not feel well. Your focus is on appropriate behavior and not on concerns of being too strict or firm.

You Clearly Communicate Your Expectations

Your decision to raise your expectations is reflected in how you relate and respond to your students (Tauber, 1999). You begin by letting the students know in plain terms exactly how you expect them to behave:

> *"You will follow all of my directions during the state test. There will be absolutely no talking during the test, and you will keep your eyes on your own paper.*

"When our visitor arrives, no disruptive behavior will be permitted. You will all sit at your desks with your eyes on our guest when he is speaking. If you want to talk, you will raise your hand and wait to be called upon.

"Because I don't feel well today, I will not tolerate any disruptive behavior from anyone. That means you will all follow each and every direction I give, the first time I give it."

You do not assume students know how you want them to behave. Instead you clearly let the students know exactly what you want them to do, and how and when you want them to do it.

You Provide More Positive Feedback and Support

Contrary to the popular belief that the only way teachers can get students to do what they want is through heavy-handed intimidation, the opposite typically occurs. On occasions when you are most effective, you go out of your way to recognize and respond to appropriate student behavior.

If you think about it, you will realize that you "heaped praise" on your students for behaving after the special guest left, expressed sincere appreciation to students for behaving when you felt ill, or offered students incentives for doing a good job on the state test.

You Are Prepared to Consistently Set Limits

While on most days you believe you have to tolerate some disruptive student behavior, when you raise the bar, you basically establish a zero-tolerance policy. In essence you are saying:

"I will not tolerate . . . students talking during the test . . . shouting out when a guest is here . . . (or) bothering me with disruptive behavior when I'm feeling so crummy."

Through your words and actions, you let students know that you "mean business" and will set and enforce limits if any student chooses to be disruptive. Your students quickly sense the change in your attitude and improve their behavior.

WHY NOT BE MORE EFFECTIVE ALL OF THE TIME?

On those occasions when you choose to raise the bar, you can influence student behavior. The issue regarding your success in managing student behavior comes down to this question:

> If I can influence my students to behave successfully on some occasions, why not choose to do so all of the time?

Chapter 5

It Is Okay to Expect Appropriate Behavior

Effective teachers believe it is appropriate to maintain high expectations for student behavior each and every day (Cipriano Pepperl & Lezotte, 2001). These teachers raise the bar from the very first day of school.

Most teachers who struggle with classroom management issues have a different perspective. They believe it is okay to be firm and expect all students to behave appropriately on state testing day, or when they feel ill, but believe it is inappropriate to expect students to behave at all other times. The question is: *Why not?*

UNREALISTIC ASSUMPTIONS

Most teachers, especially those new to the profession, have serious qualms about "coming on too strong" with their students. Teachers do not want to have to be "tough" all of the time, as shown in the examples of special occasions in the last chapter. There are three unrealistic assumptions among many educators that come from the pervasive belief that being strict will have many detrimental effects:

1. Students will not like you.

2. Students can be psychologically harmed if you are too strict.

3. Students will never learn to manage their behavior if you "sit" on them all the time.

If you believe that having such high expectations every day will harm your students or damage your relationship with them, let me assure you this will not happen. In fact, this attitude actually undermines your ability to effectively manage your classroom. Upon closer examination, you will see that this belief is unrealistic and without merit.

Unrealistic Assumption 1: Students Will Not Like You

Most teachers have been told or have read that at one time or another that their students will not like them if they are too strict. There is, of course, some truth in this statement. Being overly rigid and controlling can and will harm your relationship with your students.

Let us look at what we are really talking about on those occasions when you have effectively raised the bar. Are you asking students to be "little robots"—doing anything you command whether or not it is in their best interest? Probably not. When you raise the bar, what do you expect the students to do?

- Pay attention instead of talk when you are teaching.

- Do class work instead of disrupting the class.

- Get along with classmates instead of arguing and fighting.

These expectations are not too strict for any student. In fact, students want, need, and appreciate such clear, firm direction. Research clearly indicates:

> **Students want teachers to be firm and fair and to not allow disruptive behavior.**

Students do not like or respect teachers who let them get away with misbehavior. The foundation of student respect is based on the premise that you care enough about them to make sure they behave in a manner that is in their best interest and the best interest of others.

Unrealistic Assumption 2: Students Will Be Psychologically Harmed if You Are Too Strict

Many teachers are distressed by the overwhelming and even heart-breaking problems some of their students bring with them into the classroom. One cannot help but feel a tremendous amount of sympathy and empathy for these students.

It is natural to feel sorry for these students. As an educator, you will not want to do anything that could or would bring them further stress or harm. As a result, many teachers are very reluctant to hold these students accountable for their actions and require them to behave in the same manner as their peers. The unintended results are ultimately detrimental for the student.

> *Tanya is in a foster home and is the product of an abusive family. In the classroom, she is immature and constantly acts silly, disrupting the teacher and her classmates. Whenever the teacher sets limits on Tanya's disruptive behavior, Tanya becomes extremely upset and starts to cry. The teacher is very distressed to see how upset Tanya becomes.*

As a result, rather than setting limits on Tanya's disruptive behavior, the teacher simply tries to calm her down when she acts up. To the teacher's dismay, the other students soon start teasing Tanya about her inappropriate behavior and angrily demand to know why Tanya is allowed to not do her work and act up in class without consequences.

Though the teacher's efforts in this example are well intentioned, allowing troubled students to misbehave ultimately does much more harm than good. When you allow students to disrupt, they will eventually have difficulty in school and be labeled as "behavior problems." Students like Tanya will soon not only have to deal with the burden of being a neglected foster child, but will also experience other negative school experiences. She will not get along with peers and will gain a reputation for her immature, disruptive behavior.

One of the greatest gifts you can give students is to let them know that you know, despite their problems, that they can behave and can be successful in the classroom. These students need you to show them through your words and actions that you have high expectations for them and care enough to put the time and effort into making sure your expectations for them are ultimately reached.

Unrealistic Assumption 3: Students Will Never Learn to Manage Their Own Behavior if You "Sit" on Them All the Time

The ultimate goal of any approach to classroom management is for the students to learn self-management. Many teachers think that if they are firm or directive, students will never learn to manage their own behavior.

Research and experience clearly refute this belief. At the beginning of the school year, effective teachers are highly directive and spend extensive class time systematically teaching their students exactly how they are to behave in all classroom activities (Evertson & Harris, 1997; Witt, LaFleur, Naquin, & Gilbertson, 1999).

Effective teachers recognize this simple truth: Self-management does not just happen—it must be taught.

Will You—Or Your Students—Run Your Classroom?

If you still wonder if it is all right for you to expect your students to do what you want, consider the following question:

> Will you run your classroom or will your students run it for you?

If you do not believe it is okay to expect all of your students to meet your expectations and do what they need to do on a daily basis, then your students will end up meeting their own expectations and doing what they want to do. It is that simple!

PULLING IT ALL TOGETHER: EMPOWERING BELIEFS AND EXPECTATIONS

The foundation of your efforts to establish a classroom environment that promotes academic success begins with your beliefs and expectations. You have seen that the reality is:

- Your students can behave.

- You can influence your students to choose to behave.

- It is okay to expect your students to behave.

Classroom Management for Academic Success will help you learn the best practices that effective classroom managers use to ensure all of their students choose to behave in a manner that maximizes their academic potential.

Part 3

Teach Responsible Behavior for Academic Success at the Beginning of the School Year

Chapter 6

Part One:
Conducting a Lesson on Appropriate Behavior

Establishing a classroom environment that promotes academic success for all students begins the very first day of school. Effective teachers know that their number one priority is to take the time and effort to systematically teach students their expectations for how they are to successfully behave in all classroom activities (Evertson & Harris, 1997).

Why do effective teachers make this such a high priority? Consider the facts: Teachers who systematically teach their students classroom policies and procedures at the beginning of the year:

- Reduce disruptive behavior by 28% (Marzano et al., 2003)

- Increase time spent on instruction up to 1 hour per day (LaFleur, Witt, Naquin, Harwell, & Gilbertson, 1998)

INTRODUCTION TO TEACHING RESPONSIBLE BEHAVIOR

Your school day is made up of many specific activities such as entering the classroom, directed teaching, independent work, transitions, lining up, and even using the pencil sharpener. The specific activities and situations in the school day or period can be included in three broad categories:

1. **Instructional activities**—activities in which students will be learning, such as teacher-directed instruction and group work

2. **Procedures**—basic routines that involve movement into, within, and out of the classroom, such as transitions, lining up, and so forth

3. **Policies**—expectations that are in effect at all times in the classroom, such as classroom rules and the proper use of materials

In order to create a classroom environment that promotes academic success, you must know how you want your students to behave during specific activities and situations. Then you need to plan how you will teach them your behavioral expectations.

Effective teachers teach their students responsible behavior in the same manner as they would any academic subject (Evertson & Harris, 1997). Though there is no one way to teach appropriate behavior, the lessons of effective teachers typically follow a systematic format that addresses the needs of the different learning styles of the students.

PLANNING TO TEACH A RESPONSIBLE BEHAVIOR LESSON

Before teaching any lesson, it is important to do some planning, and the same is true for lessons on responsible behavior.

Determine the Behaviors to Be Taught

The foundation of any lesson is the behaviors you want students to learn to ensure they succeed in the activity. You will teach your students the behaviors you want to see and hear during the specific activity or situation. Use the following guidelines to determine the behaviors you want to teach.

> You will find suggested behaviors to teach for the most common instructional and procedural activities in part 7, Managing Instructional Activities to Promote Academic Success (see page 119), and part 8, Managing Procedures for Academic Success (see page 157).

Teach a limited number of behaviors. Each activity should only have three or four behaviors to learn. If there are more than four behaviors, students will have a difficult time mastering the activity.

Behaviors should be observable. Whenever possible, the behavior should be something you can see or hear, such as "Keep your hands to yourself, stay seated, and no talking." Avoid vague directions such as "Act appropriately" and "Be responsible." The clearer the direction, the more likely students will be to understand exactly what you want them to do.

Behaviors taught should include expectations regarding verbal behavior, movement, and participation. More than 90% of disruptive behavior is related to inappropriate student talking and movement and lack of student participation in the activity before them (Jones, 2000). Therefore, you need to specify the particular verbal behavior, level of movement, and participation you expect from students (see chapter 8, The Behavior Management Cycle: Step One—Effectively Communicate Explicit Directions, on page 49 for additional information).

Prepare Visual Aids

Many teachers find it helpful to use visual aids in lessons. You may want to list the behaviors being taught on an overhead transparency or a flipchart. If you use visuals, make sure they are ready before teaching the lesson. See the appendix on page 243 for overheads you might choose to use.

Teach the Lesson at the Appropriate Time

You need to teach most lessons—especially those for instructional settings and procedures—immediately before the first time you engage in the activity (see part 7, Managing Instructional Activities to Promote Academic Success, on page 119, and part 8, Managing Procedures for Academic Success, on page 157).

Many policies need to be taught during the first few days of school (see part 9, Establishing Classroom Policies for Academic Success, on page 203). Teach students the general rules for the classroom, what materials they need to bring to class each day, and other basic, though important, issues such as when they may sharpen their pencils and how they may get permission to go to the restroom.

For a day-by-day plan for scheduling your lessons, see chapter 7, Part Two: Create and Use a Beginning of the Year Responsible Behavior Curriculum, on page 37.

Determine the Amount of Time Needed to Teach Each Lesson

The time needed to teach lessons on responsible behavior will vary with the age of the students. Younger students need more time to learn the behaviors you expect from them. You should usually allocate between 5 and 10 minutes for each lesson.

RESPONSIBLE BEHAVIOR LESSON PLAN FORMAT

A lesson on responsible behavior consists of four parts:

1. Introduce the lesson.
2. Teach the behavior.
3. Model the behavior.
4. Check for understanding.

Modeling the behavior and checking for understanding can often be combined into one section.

Introduce the Lesson

Students are more motivated to learn when they understand the value the material being taught has for them. At the beginning of each lesson, you will want to tell students why it is important for them to learn how to behave responsibly during the upcoming activity. When appropriate, involve students in determining why they need to learn the behavior. For example:

> *"There will be many times in this class when you will need to work by yourself at your seat. I call this independent work. Who can tell us what the word 'independent' means?"*

Share responses.

> *"What are some things you can do independently?"*

> *"How do you feel when you do something on your own?"*

> *"Why do you think it's important to know how to work independently at school?"*

Teach the Behavior

Explain the specific behaviors you want to see and hear during the activity or situation:

> *"During independent work time, I may ask you to practice something you've just learned: to complete an assignment we began together, work on a special project, or read quietly. To be successful, you need to work on your own without talking. Stay focused on your work as though there were no distractions and as if no one else were in the room.*

> *"To help you stay focused, I expect you to follow these directions: Do only the assigned work, stay in your seat, and work without talking."*

Teach behaviors you <u>do not</u> want to see and hear. It is helpful for some students to see and hear the behaviors that you *do not* want them to do:

> *"You will not be successful if you are not doing the assigned work, out of your seat, talking, or calling out for my help."*

Model the Behavior

Modeling is a critical part of the guidance you need to give students as they learn each new skill. Modeling gives students a clear picture of what engaging in appropriate behavior looks like. Some students need to see this in order to clearly understand your expectations.

Have students model the behavior. In most lessons, you will want students to model the appropriate behavior. For example:

> *"Let's see how well some of you can act out what you've learned about working independently."*

Designate three students.

> *"We're going to pretend these three students are following directions, just like I taught you."*

Address the three students by saying:

> *"Pretend you're doing an assignment at your seat. Show us the things you should do when you're working independently."*

Some teachers find it helpful to have students briefly model the behaviors they do not want to see. It can be fun to have students "ham it up" as they model what not to do. If you have your students do this, be sure to end by having the students again model what you do want to see. The contrast leaves no doubt about how they are and are not expected to behave.

Model the behavior yourself. Another approach is to do the modeling yourself. You can easily model many situations. This approach is particularly useful with older students who may not feel it is "cool" to model appropriate behavior. For example, you could easily model both appropriate and inappropriate ways of coming into the classroom, using the pencil sharpener, and cleaning up. You may want to ham it up, especially with the inappropriate behavior. Students will love it.

Check for Understanding

One reason students have trouble learning behavioral expectations is that they may not fully understand what they are expected to do. This can be especially problematic for students who have auditory-processing problems or who are second-language learners. Make sure all students comprehend what your expectations are by checking their understanding.

Here are some techniques you will find useful. (These techniques will be helpful any time you want to review and reinforce your behavioral expectations.)

Ask students to repeat back the behaviors. Call on students and have them tell you the behaviors they are to engage in during the activity. You may want to call on students you think are having trouble following directions as a way to keep their attention. For example:

> *"Who can tell me one thing I will see or hear you do when you work on your own at your seat?"*

Signal understanding. Have students signal to you that they understand the behavior.

"If you understand what to do when I give an independent work assignment, give me a thumbs up. If you are unsure, give me a thumbs down."

Have students explain directions in their own words:

"In your own words, tell me how I expect you to behave when I give an independent work assignment."

PRACTICE AND MONITOR

What you do after you teach a lesson is as important as how effectively you taught it. As soon as you teach a lesson and students understand your behavioral expectations for a specific activity, it is important that they practice it. Like any academic subject, if it is not practiced, it may never be learned.

While students are learning and applying new behavior, it is critical that you monitor them and give them effective feedback on their performance. The Behavior Management Cycle presented in part 4 is a very useful tool that will help you give students feedback on how they are learning to behave in a responsible manner.

Chapter 7

Part Two:
Create and Use a Beginning of the Year Responsible Behavior Curriculum

Developing a behavioral curriculum you introduce at the beginning of the school year may be the single most important thing you can do to ensure student success throughout the year. Quite literally, you will be teaching students how to be successful learners.

You would not consider trying to teach students an academic topic such as reading, writing, or arithmetic without a curriculum to guide your efforts. The same is true when teaching students what is arguably the most important topic of all: how to behave responsibly during the many activities in a school day or period.

> Here is the bottom line: If the students do not learn how to behave in a responsible, nondisruptive manner throughout the day or period, you will be unable to teach them any academic subject.

Determine the Content of Your Responsible Behavior Curriculum

Developing a curriculum on any topic begins with determining what you want the students to know and be able to do. This principle also applies to teaching the students the behaviors they need to know to be successful.

To begin developing a curriculum unit on responsible behavior for academic success, you must think about the first days of school. Consider the many policies and procedures that you need students to learn to follow in order to establish a positive learning environment.

To help you in your efforts, use the following list of typical policies and procedures students need to be taught in most classrooms.

TYPICAL POLICIES AND PROCEDURES

Instructional Activities

❏ Teacher-directed instruction
❏ Whole-class discussion
❏ Sitting on the rug
❏ Independent work
❏ Working with a partner
❏ Teacher works with a small group while other students work independently
❏ Working in groups
❏ Working at centers

Procedures

❏ Attention-getting signal
❏ In-seat transitions
❏ Out-of-seat transitions
❏ Lining up to leave the classroom
❏ Walking in line
❏ Entering the classroom after recess or lunch
❏ Students going to pull-out programs
❏ Distributing and collecting materials or papers
❏ Attending an assembly
❏ Emergency drills
❏ Beginning of the day or period routine
❏ End of the day or period routine

Policies

❏ Classroom rules
❏ Positive feedback
❏ Corrective actions
❏ Bringing appropriate materials to class
❏ Making up missed work due to absence
❏ Sharpening pencils
❏ Using materials on bookshelves or in cabinets
❏ Individual students leaving class to go to the restroom
❏ Late or missing assignments
❏ Student helpers
❏ Taking care of desks, tables, and chairs
❏ Using the drinking fountain

Determine the Order of Instruction

After you determine the policies and procedures you want to teach your students, plan the order in which things will be taught. There is no single most effective order to follow when doing this, but keep the following guidelines in mind:

Teach behavioral lessons immediately before the first time the students engage in the activity. For example, just before you ask students to line up to leave the classroom for the first time, you will teach the corresponding lesson.

Teach the lesson for teacher-supervised or -directed activities before teaching lessons for student-directed activities. Structure is very important at the beginning of the year. Start by teaching behaviors for the activities over which you must have the most control.

For example, in instructional settings you should first engage in teacher-directed activities because they provide the most structure. You can then have students work independently because it is slightly less teacher-directed. The last instructional activity to present is working at centers because it is the most student-directed activity.

SAMPLE 2-WEEK CURRICULUM

Pages 41–44 provide you with a sample 2-week responsible behavior curriculum. As you review it, you may think, "When will I have time to teach?" Remember that you *are* teaching. Each lesson in the curriculum will support the academic activities you will be doing anyway. The important difference is that when you teach behavior at the same time as you engage in the activity, you provide the structure that enables students to be successful long after the 2 weeks have passed. Time spent now in this endeavor will be regained again and again. Look at this as a 2-week investment that will pay huge dividends throughout the school year.

The sample curriculum has been designed to help you plan your own 2-week responsible behavior curriculum. To help you focus on the types of lessons that need to be taught during these 2 weeks, the lessons are grouped under broad, descriptive topics. Use these as guides for focusing on issues that are most important and relevant to you and your teaching situation.

PLANNING YOUR 2-WEEK CURRICULUM

The sample curriculum that begins on page 41 can serve as a guide, but you will need to plan your own sequence of lessons based on your classroom and the activities in which you want the students to engage in. The following planning sheets will help you get organized.

Plan a Daily Schedule

Make 10 copies of the Daily Planning Sheet on page 45 (one for each day of your 2-week curriculum). Fill in the day on each copy indicating Day 1, Day 2, and so forth. Then, think about what activities you will want your students to engage in on Day 1. Using the sample curriculum as a guide, pick the appropriate lessons to teach. Write the activities down on the planning sheet for Day 1. Check off each lesson you selected on the lesson list on page 46.

Repeat this procedure for the remaining 9 days. Tag each day's lessons in this guide so that you can easily access them during class.

SAMPLE 2-WEEK CURRICULUM

DAY 1

Focus on activities that are of basic importance to you and your students right now. You need to get and hold their attention right away for these basic activities. Teaching your students the behavior you expect during less critical activities such as how to behave during an assembly can wait until later.

TOPIC: TEACHING STUDENTS TO PAY ATTENTION

Students need to learn to give you their attention immediately. They also need to learn to be active listeners whenever you are speaking.

Suggested Lessons
* Attention-Getting Signal, page 161
* Teacher-Directed Instruction, page 125

TOPIC: CLASSROOM MANAGEMENT PLAN

Teaching students your general classroom rules is an important responsibility on the first day of school.

Suggested Lessons
* Classroom Rules, page 207
* Corrective Actions, page 213
* Positive Feedback, page 210

TOPIC: STUDENT COMFORT AND SAFETY ISSUES

Students need to have their comfort issues addressed. You must also teach emergency procedures.

Suggested Lessons
* Individual Students Leaving Class to Go to the Restroom, page 230
* Using the Drinking Fountain, page 240
* Emergency Drills, page 186

TOPIC: ENDING THE DAY OR PERIOD AND LEAVING THE CLASSROOM

Students will need to be taught your end of the day procedures and how to leave the classroom.

Suggested Lessons
* End of the Day or Period Routine, page 195
* Lining up to Leave the Classroom, page 169

DAY 2

Now you will begin prioritizing behavioral expectations for other activities. Be sure to review all lessons taught the previous day to reinforce student learning.

TOPIC: INTRODUCE YOUR PROCEDURES FOR THE BEGINNING OF THE DAY OR PERIOD

The first day is usually too hectic to teach this lesson. Teaching it on the second day is very important. You will want to teach the initial procedures first and then add more procedures on later days.

Suggested Lessons
- Entering the Classroom After Recess or Lunch, page 175
- Beginning of the Day or Period Routine, page 188
- Sharpening Pencils, page 224

TOPIC: INDEPENDENT WORK

Learning to work independently is a fundamental skill that must be mastered before less teacher-directed instructional settings are attempted. Along with this instructional activity, you may also want to teach procedures that are often related to independent work, such as handling materials and in-seat transitions.

Suggested Lessons
- Independent Work, page 138
- Distributing and Collecting Materials or Papers, page 181
- In-Seat Transitions, page 163

TOPIC: OUTDOOR MANAGEMENT

The second day may be the first time that students will go to lunch and recess. Because recess and lunch procedures are almost always based on school-wide policies, specific lessons for these situations have not been included in this curriculum. However, it is important that students understand the behavioral expectations for these activities. Make sure your students understand your school's policies.

DAY 3

Review all lessons taught the previous 2 days as students engage in the activities again.

TOPIC: GROUP DISCUSSIONS

This is a step down from the highly structured, teacher-directed, independent-work activity. In the following lesson, students will be taught how to participate in a discussion.

Suggested Lesson
- Whole-Class Discussion, page 130

TOPIC: USE OF CLASSROOM SPACE

When students start moving around the room, they need to know your expectations for using different areas of the classroom, including their own desks and yours.

Suggested Lessons
- Using Materials on Bookshelves or in Cabinets, page 227
- Taking Care of Desks, Tables, and Chairs, page 238

TOPIC: END OF THE SCHOOL DAY OR PERIOD

By the end of the third day, students have enough skills to begin learning to take more responsibility in the classroom. Students should be taught how to complete student helper tasks, take down homework assignments, and get the classroom ready for the next day.

Suggested Lesson
- Student Helpers, page 235

DAY 4

Review all of the lessons from the previous days as you repeat the activities. Focus new lessons on key recurring activities that have not yet been covered.

TOPIC: MORE PROCEDURES FOR THE BEGINNING OF THE DAY OR PERIOD

Students should be ready by this point to learn the rest of the procedures for the beginning of the day or period.

Suggested Lessons
- Bringing Appropriate Materials to Class, page 218
- Making up Missed Work Due to Absence, page 221
- Late or Missing Assignments, page 232

DAY 5

By the fifth day, students will need a day of review. Instead of teaching new lessons, spend the day reviewing those you have taught, especially those covered during the last 2 days.

DAY 6

The lessons suggested for the first days of school focus largely on individual student responsibilities. Now you can begin to teach your expectations for more complex activities where students need to demonstrate responsible behavior in situations with less teacher-directed activity.

TOPIC: WORKING WITH A PARTNER

Working in pairs is the most structured learning activity that involves students working together. Students need to learn how to work with one other student before they are asked to work in a group.

Suggested Lesson
- Working With a Partner, page 142

DAY 7

Continue to review previous lessons. The topics that follow over the next few days should be taught in the order shown to help students build skills that will enable them to be successful in instructional settings that require more responsibility and self-management. Depending on your own classroom situation, it may be appropriate to teach these lessons in future weeks when the students are prepared for more independent activities.

TOPIC: STUDENTS WORK INDEPENDENTLY WHILE THE TEACHER IS WITH A SMALL GROUP

By the fourth day, students should have learned how to work independently. You can then introduce the much less structured situation in which the teacher works with a small group while other students work independently at their seats.

Suggested Lesson

- Teacher Works With a Small Group While Other Students Work Independently, page 146

DAY 8

Review lessons from the previous 2 days, but also make sure that students continue to meet the expectations taught during the first days of school.

TOPIC: WORKING IN COOPERATIVE GROUPS

Cooperative group activities should be taught only after students have learned how to pay attention, work with a partner, move around the room, and get and use materials. Do not attempt these activities until you are sure they have learned how to behave in other less teacher-directed activities. Working in cooperative groups is a highly complex activity. Start slowly, focusing first on transitioning to the group and then on behaving within the group.

Suggested Lesson

- Working in Groups, page 150

DAY 9

Review lessons from the previous day and continue teaching students how to work in cooperative groups.

TOPIC: WORKING AT LEARNING CENTERS

Teach students how to use a learning center before you send them there for an activity. Start by instructing them on how to use two simple centers. After the students have mastered going to these centers, add more as appropriate. Make sure you are free to monitor students while they are at the centers.

Suggested Lesson

- Working at Centers, page 153

DAY 10

Students will need a day of review. Determine which lessons need reinforcement and work with students on improving their skills.

TEACHING RESPONSIBLE BEHAVIOR DAILY PLANNING SHEET

Day _____

List the lessons you plan to teach and the page on which each lesson begins. Add any notes or reminders that will help you organize and teach the lesson.

1. _____ Page ____

2. _____ Page ____

3. _____ Page ____

4. _____ Page ____

5. _____ Page ____

6. _____ Page ____

7. _____ Page ____

8. _____ Page ____

9. _____ Page ____

10. _____ Page ____

TEACHING RESPONSIBLE BEHAVIOR LESSON LIST

Instructional Settings Lessons

- ❏ Teacher-Directed Instruction
- ❏ Whole-Class Discussion
- ❏ Sitting on the Rug
- ❏ Independent Work
- ❏ Working With a Partner
- ❏ Teacher Works with a Small Group While Other Students Work Independently
- ❏ Working in Groups
- ❏ Working at Centers

Procedures Lessons

- ❏ Attention-Getting Signal
- ❏ In-Seat Transitions
- ❏ Out-of-Seat Transitions
- ❏ Lining Up to Leave the Classroom
- ❏ Walking in Line
- ❏ Entering the Classroom After Recess or Lunch
- ❏ Students Going to Pull-Out Programs
- ❏ Distributing and Collecting Materials or Papers
- ❏ Attending an Assembly
- ❏ Emergency Drills
- ❏ Beginning of the Day or Period Routine
- ❏ End of the Day or Period Routine

Policies Lessons

- ❏ Classroom Rules
- ❏ Positive Feedback
- ❏ Corrective Actions
- ❏ Bringing Appropriate Materials to Class
- ❏ Making Up Missed Work Due to Absence
- ❏ Sharpening Pencils
- ❏ Using Materials on Bookshelves or in Cabinets
- ❏ Individual Students Leaving Class to Go to the Restroom
- ❏ Late or Missing Assignments
- ❏ Student Helpers
- ❏ Taking Care of Desks, Tables, and Chairs
- ❏ Students Going to Pull-Out Program
- ❏ Using the Drinking Fountain

Part 4

The Behavior Management Cycle

Chapter 8

The Behavior Management Cycle
Step One—Effectively Communicate Explicit Directions

Teaching procedures and policies at the beginning of the year is the first step in laying the foundation for a classroom environment that promotes academic success (Evertson & Harris, 1997). Through this process, you will introduce your students to your expectations for how they are to behave in the numerous activities in each school period or day.

Effective teachers recognize that the next step in creating a positive, disruption-free classroom environment is to systematically reinforce the need for students to meet expectations for appropriate behavior at all times in the classroom (Jones, 2000). The goal is to minimize the time spent on disruptive, nonproductive student behavior and to maximize the time spent on instruction.

Effective teachers know that in order to increase the time available for learning, they must be able to motivate students to quickly follow directions and to get and stay on task. The importance of all students following teacher directions cannot be underestimated.

> The foundation of managing classroom behavior rests upon your ability to motivate students to simply follow your directions.

What happens when you give directions to students—such as "Take out your books and get to work without talking"—and some students start fooling around and talking? Do you have behavior problems that will interfere with student learning? Of course you do.

On the other hand, if all students follow your directions by taking out their books and getting to work, do you have behavior problems? Of course not. The fundamental importance of following teacher directions is that simple.

THE BEHAVIOR MANAGEMENT CYCLE

How can you improve your ability to get all of your students to follow directions and quickly get and stay on task?

The Behavior Management Cycle is a systematic approach that will help you motivate your students to quickly follow your directions, thus maximizing instruction time. This sequence begins whenever you give directions to the students:

The following sections of this handbook present the theoretical and practical foundations for effectively using the Behavior Management Cycle in your efforts with students.

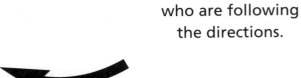

Step One: Effectively communicate the explicit directions you expect students to follow.

Step Two: Use behavioral narration to support students who are following the directions.

Step Three: Take corrective action with students who are still not complying with the directions.

STEP ONE: EFFECTIVELY COMMUNICATE EXPLICIT DIRECTIONS

The first step in motivating your students to follow your directions is to make sure that the directions you give are clear and precise—that is, your directions should be explicit (Riegler & Baer, 1989). Research indicates that explicit directions are critical to reducing the disruptive behavior of students (Walker & Walker, 1991). (Please note that in many instances, the directions you give students may be similar or the same as those you presented in the lessons you taught at the beginning of the year. See part 3, beginning on page 29.)

Vague Versus Explicit Directions

Teachers who struggle with classroom management issues often give unclear or vague directions to their students. Vague directions are those that do not explicitly communicate to students exactly *how* you want them to behave in order to be successful during an activity.

Explicit directions, on the other hand, communicate to students exactly how they are to behave to successfully engage in the classroom activity.

Vague Directions:

"I want everyone to take your chair to your study group and wait for my directions."

Explicit Directions:

"I want everyone to quietly pick up your chair and, without talking, walk directly to your study group, sit down, and wait for my directions on how to do your assignment."

Vague Directions:

"I need everyone to pay attention."

Explicit Directions:

"I need everyone's attention. That means your eyes are on me, there is nothing in your hands but your pencil, and no one is talking."

Vague Directions:

"I want you to begin working with your partner on the questions on page 14."

Explicit Directions:

"When I say GO, I want you to take out your workbooks and immediately begin working with your partner on the questions on page 14. Use your indoor voices."

Realistic Expectations

Like many teachers, you may honestly believe that you should not have to constantly give such explicit directions to your students. You may be thinking:

"I teach the students how I want them to behave at the beginning of the year and that is all I should have to do."

"My students are old enough that they should know how to behave without me having to direct them all the time."

Since almost all of your students live up to your expectations—whether they simply want to please you, are self-directed, or are compliant by nature—you come to believe that your expectations are valid, right? No! The reality is that your expectations for what most students need will likely not be effective with your noncompliant students. The following scenario helps illustrate this point:

> *Stephen is a highly disruptive, noncompliant student. When the class is in the middle of a journal writing assignment, he returns to the classroom after working with the special education teacher. The teacher sees him at the door and tells him, "Stephen, I want you to go to your seat and get to work on your journal." She turns to help another student with her assignment and soon notices Stephen slowly walk toward his seat, poking and teasing several students as he passes by them. He finally sits down and starts talking and fooling around with the students around him. Stephen eventually starts working on his journal for a second or two, but soon is back to talking with his classmates.*
>
> *Completely frustrated, the teacher thinks to herself, "Oh no, there he goes again. He should know how to behave by now. He simply wears me out!" Out of patience, she says, "Stephen, cut it out. You know better than to act that way. Either get to work or you'll be sorry."*

Let's dissect the directions the teacher gave Stephen and his response to them. This process will help you understand why you must be explicit rather than vague when giving instructions to noncompliant students.

The teacher's directions to Stephen were:

- *"Go to your seat."*
- *"Get to work on your journal."*

Stephen's response: Technically, he did "follow the directions." He:

- Went to his seat
- Took out his journal and began to work

The problem was *how* he went to his seat and started work.

Since he was not told explicitly *how* to go to his seat with a directive statement such as "Go directly to your seat without bothering any other students," he chose how he wanted to get there—by taking his time and provoking other students. The same is true for *how* he got to work. Again, he was not given explicit instructions about how to begin working so he chose to accomplish the task with much talking and fooling around.

A major mistake teachers make with noncompliant students is to *assume* they know how they are *expected* to behave, as most other students do. As shown in the previous scenario, teachers who assume this often give *vague* directions that should be enough but simply are not.

The problem with giving vague directions to noncompliant students can be understood if we consider the earlier discussion on how these students are different from their classmates.

> Remember, noncompliant students have a strong desire to do what they want, when they want, and how they want. If they feel they have a choice, they will often choose to do what they want instead of what you want them to do.

When your directions are vague rather than explicit, noncompliant students often decide that you are not clear on exactly what you want them to do, so they can try to do what they want. As a result, these students will frequently test you by doing what they want and watching for your reaction.

To reduce your frustration with noncompliant students, you should recognize the following reality:

> Noncompliant students often will not respond to the vague directions that work for most of your students. Noncompliant students need to be told explicitly what they are to do whenever you give directions.

A final quick aside: When you make your directions more explicit, you will probably find that many of your students benefit from your added specificity. Many students have various learning issues. When you make your directions more specific, you will make it easier for all of your students to succeed in your classroom.

Guidelines for Determining Explicit Directions

Explicit directions communicate to the students the exact behavior you expect them to engage in to be successful during the upcoming activity. The directions typically need to include your expectations for student verbal behavior, physical movement, and participation (Witt et al., 1999).

Verbal behavior. Up to 80% of the disruptive behavior of your students can be categorized as one form or another of inappropriate verbal behavior (Jones, 2000). Thus, whenever you give directions to your students, you need to explicitly know and communicate what verbal behavior is expected.

- *"No talking."*

- *"Use your '12-inch indoor voice.'"*

- *"Raise your hand and wait to be called on before you speak."*

Physical movement. Approximately 15% of the disruptive behavior of your students involves inappropriate movement (Jones, 2000). Thus, the second area in which you need to know and communicate what behavior you expect when you give directions relates to student movement.

- *"Stay in your seat."*

- *"Walk—do not run."*

- *"Go directly to your seat."*

Participation in activity. In most activities you ask students to engage in, you need to know how you want them to participate in order to be successful. Thus, the third area in which you need to know what behavior you expect is how you want students to participate in the activity.

- *"Get right to work."*

- *"Do your own work."*

- *"Take turns with your partner."*

Here are additional examples of explicit directions:

"I'm going to be going over the new math concepts I told you about. Everyone needs to take out your math workbooks and turn to page 84. There is no need for anyone to get out of their seat or to talk until I ask for questions."

"It is time to line up for recess. Quietly put away all of your materials. When I call your table, I want you to quietly push in your chair, walk directly to the end of the line, and stand with your hands to yourself without talking."

Guidelines for Effectively Giving Explicit Directions

There are some basic guidelines that effective teachers follow when giving directions to their students (Canter & Canter, 2001a).

Have the attention of all of your students. Make sure that all of your students pay attention whenever you give directions. This may be a challenge with noncompliant students. Here are strategies that can enable you to get the attention of all of your students.

Verbal cues to get student attention. When you have students who tend not to pay attention when you give directions, one way to let them know you expect them to listen to and follow your directions is to cue them by name. That is, when you give the directions, you cue the noncompliant students to the fact that you expect them to follow your directions.

> *"I'm going to want everyone—including Jerome, Carlin, and Cheryl—to go directly to your seat, take out the book, and immediately get to work without talking."*

Physical clues to get student attention. You can also cue the students through your physical actions. A great way to get your students' attention when you are giving directions is to simply stand by them when you are talking. Your proximity sends a clear message to the students that you are aware of them and their behavior.

Another simple physical cue is to look at particular students and make eye contact while delivering your directions. When you make eye contact with a student, you will have his or her attention and the student will be more likely to listen to and follow your directions.

Model appropriate behavior. Another strategy to get and keep the attention of students who tend to be off task is to have them model for the class how to follow your directions. As the students are modeling, narrate what they are doing:

> *"I would like Carlin and Jerome to show everyone what they are to do next."*

The students begin to model how to follow the directions.

> *"Carlin and Jerome are walking directly to their seats. They are taking out their books and getting right to work, and they're doing all of this with no talking. This is exactly what I want to see everyone do. That was excellent."*

Another benefit of having students model how to follow the directions is that you are assured that these students will be able to follow the directions successfully.

Check for understanding. Whenever you give directions to students, it is important to check to see if all the students understand the directions. Noncompliant students may often also have learning issues that make it harder for them to comprehend your directions. You can use various strategies to determine if students understand your directions:

> *Have students repeat back the directions.* Call on students (particularly students who have trouble following directions—when appropriate), and have

them repeat back to you the behaviors they are expected to engage in during the upcoming activity.

"I'm going to call on students and have them tell me one behavior I want to see and hear when I tell you to go back to your seats."

Have students signal understanding. Ask students to indicate if they do or do not understand the directions.

"If you understand the directions, give me a thumbs up. If you don't, give me a thumbs down."

Cue the students to start the activity. Often when you give directions to the students, they will begin the activity before you are ready for them to do so. Be sure to always tell the students when they should begin.

"I do not want anyone to start the activity until I say GO."

PULLING IT ALL TOGETHER

We have just examined the first step of the Behavior Management Cycle: Effectively communicate explicit directions. In order to effectively communicate your expectations, remember:

- You cannot assume your students know how to behave appropriately.

- Your students must know every second of every school day what you expect from them.

- Before beginning any activity, you need to give your students the explicit directions you want them to follow.

- Whenever you give directions to students, you need to make sure they are all paying attention and understand what they are to do.

Chapter 9 discusses the second step of the Behavior Management Cycle: using behavioral narration.

Chapter 9

The Behavior Management Cycle
Step Two—Using Behavioral Narration

In the first step of the Behavior Management Cycle, you clearly communicate to students the directions for how they are expected to behave. The next obvious question becomes: How do you influence all of the students—especially those who have been noncompliant—to quickly follow the directions and get on task?

REALISTIC EXPECTATIONS

Most teachers I work with who struggle with classroom management issues sincerely believe one or more of the following statements:

- *"Students **should** just want to follow my directions because that is the right thing to do."*

- *"I **should** not have to waste my time and energy doing anything to motivate my students to follow directions."*

- *"When I give directions, the students **should** follow them. If they don't, I'll just get after them!"*

In theory, I agree that all of your students *should* just follow your directions. In fact, this belief is probably reinforced by the fact that most of your students simply follow your directions without any additional motivation on your part. The issue we are dealing with again is that *most* of the students is obviously not the same as *all* of them.

If, from your point of view, you think students should simply follow your directions without additional encouragement, will you be motivated to do more than simply give directions? No, you will not. As you will see, the consequences of this belief will be negative for you and your students.

What happens when you expect that students *should* simply follow your directions and they do not? Let us look at a typical scenario in which you would give directions to your students:

"When I say GO, I want everyone to go directly back to their seats, take out their books, and get to work without any talking. Okay, ready, GO!"

Most of the students quickly comply, but a few as usual do not. Out of frustration, you respond to those students:

"Steve, the direction was to go back to your seat—come on now. Marsha, I've had it with you—get to work. It isn't time to talk. Carlos, what's wrong with you? Stop fooling around. What is wrong with you kids? Why can't you ever just follow my directions?"

When you expect students to follow your directions and they do not, you will naturally become upset and may tend to nag the students to do what you want. No one likes nagging. You end up feeling like a "shrew" who is constantly harping on the students, and the students do not like the negative tone that is set by your constant badgering.

There is another unintended consequence of expecting students to simply follow your directions. If you expect that students *should* follow your directions, why bother putting in any effort encouraging them to do so? Thus, you will rarely respond to students who comply with your directions. In other words, you will basically ignore them.

What is the impact of ignoring students who follow your directions? You send a clear message to your students: "If you want my attention, you will not get it by following my directions. You will need to misbehave." This message is particularly detrimental to those students who have a hard time following your directions and may need your attention. You may actually be reinforcing or motivating these students to do exactly what you do not want them to do.

To reduce your frustration, set a more positive tone in the classroom, and motivate students to do what you want, you need to reexamine your expectation that *all students should simply follow your directions.* The reality is this:

> You have noncompliant students who will not simply follow your directions without additional encouragement and motivation to do so.

The question then becomes: How can you effectively motivate them to do what you want?

BEHAVIORAL NARRATION

A key to motivating students to follow your directions is to give them *effective* positive feedback.

> Research indicates that teachers who provide effective positive feedback can reduce disruptive behavior by over 30% (Stage & Quiroz, 1997).

In over 30 years of working with teachers, the most effective type of positive feedback I have observed is what I call *behavioral narration*. Here is how behavioral narration works: When you finish giving directions to the students, you immediately monitor the class and look for students who *are complying*. Then, in a voice loud enough for the class to hear, you simply narrate, or describe, what you see them doing.

"When I say GO, I want everyone to go directly back to their seats, take out their books, and immediately get to work—and I want you to do this without talking. I'll be looking for students who are following my directions. Ready, GO!"

Behavioral narration:
"Mary is going directly back to her seat without talking. Meredith has taken out her book and is already getting to work. Alberto has gone back to his seat, taken out his book, and is working without talking."

Since middle- and secondary-level students often do not want to be singled out by their teachers for "being good," with older students, you will want to narrate the behavior of groups of students who are following your directions.

Behavioral narration:
"I see the students at table four are walking to their seats without talking. Students at table three already have their books out. Students at table five are working without talking."

Why is this simple strategy such an effective motivator to help you influence all of your students to follow your directions? Let us take a closer look at the benefits of using behavioral narration.

Behavioral Narration Enables You to Repeat Directions in a Positive Manner

When you use behavioral narration, you are basically *repeating* your directions to students by describing the behavior of those students who are following your directions.

Direction: *"Go directly back to your seat."*
Behavioral narration: *"Mary is going directly back to her seat."*

Direction: *"Take out your book and get immediately to work."*
Behavioral narration: *"Marsha has taken out her book and has already started to work."*

Direction: *"I want you to do this without talking."*
Behavioral narration: *"Alberto is working without talking."*

Some students may have difficulty following your directions if you only give them once. That is, some of your students who act noncompliant may in reality have learning issues that make it more difficult for them to process your directions. In addition, these students may not have been listening when you initially gave the directions and will have trouble following them even if they want to.

It is therefore necessary to often repeat your directions to help some students successfully follow them. In fact, you probably already repeat your directions often. The previous scenario shows how you may typically do so in a negative manner: "Come on now, I don't want to have to tell you again. I said, 'Go back to your seats and get to work.'"

The value of using behavioral narration is that it enables you to consistently repeat your directions in a positive manner: "James is going back to his seat and getting right to work." This strategy will enable you to go from *badgering* students to follow your directions to *encouraging* them to do so.

Behavioral Narration Enables You to Motivate Students Without the Drawbacks of Praise

Many teachers confuse behavioral narration with praise. Though both can be used to motivate students to follow directions, behavioral feedback can prove significantly more useful. It is a particularly good tool for those students who continue to frustrate you.

Praise is judgmental—behavioral narration is descriptive. When you praise students, you are making a judgmental statement about their behavior:

"I like the way Matt went back to his seat."

"Nina is doing a good job of working without talking."

"Lety has her book out and is working quietly—that is what I like to see."

Such judgmental statements by their nature encourage students to do what you want in order to get your approval, and this is problematic for several reasons (Kohn, 1993; Tauber, 1999). First, if your goal is to teach students to be self-motivated, the constant use of such judgmental, approval-seeking comments sends a message to the students that they are to behave not for their own benefit but for your acceptance. Second, some students could care less about pleasing you. In fact, they may not want your approval. You have probably had the experience of praising students for their appropriate behavior only to have them turn around and do exactly what you did not want them to do. Praising students can often backfire.

Behavioral narration is *descriptive*. When you use behavioral narration, you simply verbalize what you are observing the students doing. For example:

"Tanya walked to her seat, took out her book, and is working without talking."

By simply describing what you are seeing and hearing, you are giving positive, nonjudgmental recognition that can serve as a powerful motivator for most students.

Excessive praise sounds inauthentic. Praising students is a valuable tool you can use to motivate them to do what you want. As the old saying goes, "One can get too much of a good thing." If you are constantly stating how much you like what the students are doing or what a good job they have done or how proud you are of how they are behaving, eventually several problems will develop. First, you will find yourself sounding so "syrupy sweet" that you probably will not be able to stand it. Second, many students will eventually realize that you praise everything students do. The value of your comments will diminish dramatically.

In contrast, behavioral narration is merely a description of on-task student behavior. Given the matter-of-fact nature of behavioral narration, you will find you can use it consistently without feeling phony. Even more important, students will not likely tire of your positive comments and will continue to be motivated by them.

Behavioral narration demonstrates to your students that you are on top of their behavior in a positive manner. A fundamental tenet of classroom management is that you, the teacher, need to be able to consistently demonstrate to all of the students that you are *on top of* what is going on in the classroom and are prepared to make sure students comply with your directions. Why is this so important?

Students are *always* watching you to determine if they have to listen to you or can choose to do what they want. The more they are convinced you are on top of what is going on, the more likely they will be to choose to listen to your wishes as opposed to "doing their own thing."

Most teachers have been led to believe that the way to demonstrate that they are on top of student behavior is to consistently monitor the classroom for students who are not following directions and then to quickly and firmly respond to their off-task behavior. The problem with this approach, as we have observed, is that teachers find themselves constantly having to correct students with statements such as "Amy, don't do that" and "Adrian, get to work." These kinds of statements will set a negative tone in a classroom.

Here is the dilemma you face: How do you demonstrate to students you are on top of their behavior without being negative? The answer to this question is another major benefit of using behavioral narration.

> *Immediately after you give directions, actively monitor and clearly narrate the behavior of students who are on task:*
>
> *"I see Zach is going back to his seat and Josh is already getting to work and is not talking."*
>
> *By monitoring and narrating behavior, you will send a clear message to all students that you are aware of what is going on and definitely on top of how they are behaving.*

The consistent use of behavioral narration gives you the opportunity to demonstrate to your students that you are on top of their behavior in a positive manner. This method not only motivates students to follow your directions but begins to change the entire climate in your classroom! The impact created when badgering stops and encouragement with positive recognition begins cannot be underestimated.

How to Use Behavioral Narration to Get All of Your Students to Follow Directions and to Get on Task

There are various guidelines to follow for ensuring your effectiveness in using behavioral narration to get all of your students to follow your directions and get on task.

Use behavioral narration immediately after giving your directions—The "2-Second Rule." After giving directions to your students, your number one priority needs to be to follow the 2-Second Rule.

The 2-Second Rule

Immediately after completing any directions, begin monitoring student compliance. Within 2 seconds, begin narrating the behavior of students who are on task.

Do not allow yourself to be distracted by preparing to conduct the lesson or by such things as students asking questions. If you do not follow the 2-second rule to begin narrating on-task student behavior, your students may sense that you are not on top of what is going on, and they will begin to test your authority.

Describe the behavior of at least three students. After you give your directions, you will want to describe the behavior of at least three students who are complying (Colvin & Lazer,

1997). By following this guideline, you will ensure two important and positive results. First, you have sufficiently repeated the directions to ensure that all students understand them. Second, you have let students know you are on top of their behavior.

Monitor students who have difficulty following directions. You will always need to keep an eye on students who have difficulty following directions to determine if they are on task. Doing this will enable you to accomplish two goals.

First, when you look at students—and especially when you make eye contact—you let them know you are fully aware of their behavior. For most students, this eye contact will increase the probability that they will do what you want.

Second, if you are monitoring a particular student's behavior and he or she *does* follow your directions, you will have an opportunity to narrate the behavior and that will further motivate the student to behave appropriately.

Use behavioral narration before you correct student behavior. Some students may not immediately comply when you give directions. Again, resist the temptation to correct their behavior until you have narrated the behavior of three on-task students. This will only take a few seconds and may be sufficient to positively cue the off-task students to get on task. The next chapter addresses what you need to do if students still choose not to follow your directions—even after you have used behavioral narration.

There are obviously exceptions to the guideline to try behavioral narration before you correct a student. For example, if a student becomes extremely disruptive by screaming out, hitting another student, and so forth, you would not ignore this behavior to simply narrate the on-task behavior of another student. When students are so disruptive that their behavior interferes with the functioning of the classroom, you will have to immediately correct it.

Use behavioral narration as frequently as necessary. When you begin using behavioral narration, use it *every time* you give your directions. Most teachers find that this simple change in how they manage behavior has a dramatic effect on the classroom.

Over time you can phase out the frequency of how often you use behavioral narration. The key criteria to determine the frequency that you use the strategy is directly related to the level of off-task or disruptive behavior you encounter. As long as you have students who do not follow directions, you need to continue using behavioral narration.

With some classes you can phase out the use of the strategy after a month or two, and with others you may need to use behavioral narration the entire year.

How to Use Behavioral Narration to Keep Students on Task

When you use behavioral narration, you will find that you can more effectively motivate your students to get on task in all class activities. Behavioral narration is also a highly effective tool to help you handle another frustrating problem: keeping students on task during any instructional activity, no matter if you are teaching a lesson, students are working independently, or students are working in groups.

Why is it so difficult to keep students on task during an instructional activity? You have probably experienced these scenarios:

You begin teaching a lesson and have everyone's attention only to find that within a few minutes some students start "zoning out" or talking. Soon more and more students follow their lead.

Students begin working independently and work quietly, but soon some start to talk. A "low buzz" begins, and in no time it seems as though more students are talking and fooling around than working.

Let us examine how you can use behavioral narration to motivate all students to stay engaged and on task.

Consistently narrate the behavior of students who are staying on task—Use the "1-Minute Rule." When your students are engaged in an instructional activity, you need to make managing their behavior a top priority (Jones, 2000). Thus, during any instructional activity, you need to make sure you monitor the students' behavior and, as needed, narrate the behavior of students who are staying on task.

As a rule of thumb, when you first start teaching students how to stay on task during an instructional activity, you will want to follow the 1-Minute Rule in which you monitor student behavior once a minute and narrate the behavior of on-task students (see feature box on page 65).

Through the consistent narration of students who are staying on task, you accomplish three things. First, you provide a clear reminder to students of what you expect them to be doing. Second, you again send a message that you are on top of the behavior you want. Finally, you are able to motivate students in a positive way to stay on task throughout the lesson.

Follow the remaining guidelines for using behavioral narration to get students on task. When using behavioral narration to motivate students to stay on task, most of the guidelines presented in the previous section apply. You need to use behavioral narration to narrate the behavior of at least three students who are staying on task before you correct students.

The 1-Minute Rule

During an instructional activity, monitor student behavior at least once a minute and narrate the behavior of the students who are staying on task.

The following scenarios show the 1-minute rule in action.

- *You are conducting a teacher-directed lesson with the class. Every time you finish a point, you scan the class and narrate students who are engaged in the lesson: "Will, Josh, and Estavan have their eyes on me, are paying attention, and are not talking."*

- *Your students are working independently on an assignment. As you walk around the room, you stop after helping each student to narrate students who are staying on task: "Daniel and Jerome are working on their assignment without talking. Maria has finished her assignment and has quietly walked over and picked out a free reading book."*

- *You are working with a small reading group while other students work independently at their seats. As you finish reading with each student, you look up, monitor the class, and narrate students who are staying on task: "Kishan, Abdul, and Alana are still in their seats and are reading without talking."*

When Appropriate, Use Behavioral Narration With a Points-on-the-Board Classwide Reward System

Some teachers find that an effective strategy to further increase the impact of behavioral narration is to combine it with a classwide reward system (Marzano et al., 2003). A class-wide reward system is a program that motivates all of your students to work together to earn a reward for the entire class. Typical rewards might include free time, a homework-free night, a special treat, and so on.

One of the most effective classwide reward systems is called *points-on-the-board*. In this system you establish a goal for the number of points the class must earn to get a reward. Whenever you see students following your directions, you not only narrate the behavior, but you also let the class know the students have earned a point that will move the class closer to its reward.

> *"Juan is going back to his seat and Kris has started working. Allie is working without talking, and they have earned a point for the class."*

A points-on-the-board system enables you to motivate older students to get and stay on task. By combining behavioral narration with a points-on-the-board classwide reward system, you can increase its effectiveness in controlling classroom discipline, especially with older students.

If you teach adolescents, you may be thinking that most if not all of your students would be embarrassed if you used behavioral narration to single them out for doing what you want. The last thing any adolescent wants is to be seen as a "goody-goody" in front of peers.

The way around this dilemma is to make sure that when you single students out, you make it clear to their classmates that they are earning points toward the class reward. Students will not mind your narrating their appropriate behavior if they are helping their classmates reach a reward that they all want.

A points-on-the-board reward system used with a little savvy can also be an invaluable tool for motivating noncompliant students who have not responded to any strategy you have tried in the past. The key to using this reward system to motivate these students is to make sure you are constantly looking for them to be on task.

Whenever you spot these students following the directions, you immediately narrate their behavior and give a point toward the class reward. As a result, these students will end up earning more points for the class than other students! The impact of this can be dramatic.

As was stated, many adolescent students are not motivated by your recognition. Therefore, the use of behavioral narration alone will rarely be effective. But when you make sure that noncompliant students can earn more points than other students toward a reward all students want, the class will soon catch on.

You will often find classmates will take these students aside and say, in effect, "The teacher gives you points every time you follow directions. The more you follow directions, the sooner we'll get the class reward, so *do* follow directions!" We all know how powerful a motivator this kind of peer pressure can be for adolescents.

Guidelines for using points on the board. The following basic guidelines will help you effectively use a points-on-the-board classwide reward system.

Determine the class reward. Identify a reward that the students will want to earn. This reward must meet two criteria: You must be comfortable having the students earn it, and it must be a reward that students truly want and are willing to work for. Possible rewards include:

- Extra free time
- Extra physical education time

- Special activity

- Class party

- Skip a homework assignment

- Special treat like popcorn or another snack

- Listen to music in class

Make sure students earn the reward quickly. It is critical that you make sure that your students earn the reward quickly. The number one reason this reward system fails to motivate students is the teacher makes it too hard for students to earn a reward, and the students lose interest in it. The appropriate time span students can wait to earn the reward varies by grade level, so use the following guidelines for earning the reward to keep your students interested:

- **Grades K–1** 1 day

- **Grades 2–3** 2 days to 1 week

- **Grades 4–5** 1 week

- **Grades 6–8** 1 to 2 weeks

After the class has earned a reward, identify the next class reward. As long as your students need an extra incentive, continue using a classwide reward system to reinforce your behavior management strategies.

Students need to earn points frequently throughout the period or day. For this reward system to be motivating, students need to receive points on a constant basis while in class.

A good rule of thumb is that students need to earn at least 10 points per hour, or approximately 50 points per day.

That means that you have to be constantly looking for students who are following your directions, narrating their behavior, and giving out points. It may seem like it is a lot of points that would interfere with your instruction, but as long as the goals are reasonable, the more points you give, the quicker your behavior problems will diminish. Thus, if the students earn 50 points a day and need to earn the reward in 3 days, for example, the point goal for the reward is 150 points.

An important word of warning:

Never take away points the students have earned.

All too often a frustrated teacher will take away class points because of the disruptive behavior of some students. This can easily backfire by frustrating the students. A teacher who has a particularly bad day could have the students end up *owing* points, not *earning* points. If this happened, student motivation would drop considerably.

Establish a points corner in a prominent location. Determine a place on the board where you will record points when students earn them. Make sure you can easily reach the location. If appropriate, sometimes have students record the points when they are earned.

Systematically introduce the points-on-the-board reward system to the students. If you decide to use a points-on-the-board reward system, be sure to carefully explain it to the students in detail. Tell students why you are using the program, what reward they can earn, and how they can earn it:

> *"I have an idea that I think can help everyone learn to follow directions and be successful in this classroom. You have been constantly asking for more free time during class. I have a way for everyone to earn 15 minutes of extra free time. Here is how it works.*

> *"Whenever I give directions, I will look for students who are following them. When I see students following directions, I will recognize their behavior and they will earn a point for the class that I will mark on the board. When the class earns 100 points, you will get 15 extra minutes of free time at the end of that day.*

> *"The more I see students following directions, the more points you will get and the quicker you will earn your extra free time."*

When you finish explaining the points-on-the-board system, encourage students to ask questions to make sure they understand the details of how it will work.

PULLING IT ALL TOGETHER

We have examined the second step of the Behavior Management Cycle: using behavioral narration. In order to effectively use this strategy, remember:

- You cannot expect some of your students to simply want to follow your directions without additional motivation.

- When used according to the guidelines presented, behavioral narration can be a highly effective strategy to motivate all students to follow your directions, get on task, and stay on task.

The next chapter focuses on the third step of the Behavior Management Cycle: taking corrective action.

Chapter 10

The Behavior Management Cycle
Step Three—Take Corrective Action

When you have followed the first two steps of the Behavior Management Cycle—that is, you have clearly given explicit directions and used behavioral narration—but continue to have students who are off task or disruptive, you will need to implement the third step: Take corrective action. Corrective actions—be they directive verbal statements or disciplinary consequences—are used to motivate students to stop their off-task, disruptive behavior.

No area in the field of classroom management is more controversial than the use of corrective actions. Many so-called experts claim such actions are basically ineffective, if not harmful. Research and experience tell us otherwise:

> Effective use of disciplinary consequences can reduce disruptive behavior in a classroom by close to 30% (Stage & Quiroz, 1997).
>
> When used effectively, disciplinary consequences reduce disruptive behavior at all grade levels (Marzano et al., 2003).

HOW TO EFFECTIVELY TAKE CORRECTIVE ACTION

Effective teachers use the following strategies to successfully motivate students to stop their disruptive behavior and to get and stay on task.

Follow the 10-Second Rule

When you give directions to students and one or more students do not follow them, how many students are aware that these few students are not listening to you? Most likely, all of them!

The reality is that when you give directions, students are always watching to see if you are or are not going to correct the misbehavior of their classmates. If they see you will not correct the other students' behavior, they will interpret this as a clear message that you are not on top of what is going on and that they can misbehave as well (Witt et al., 1999).

The 10-Second Rule

Within 10 seconds after you give directions, you will need to effectively correct the off-task, disruptive behavior of students.

You have only 10 seconds after you finish giving your directions and cue the students to follow them to correct any off-task or disruptive students. If you do not do so, you will soon find other students who will join their off-task classmates, eventually resulting in a "pack" of off-task, disruptive students (Kounin, 1970).

You may wonder how you will have time to use behavioral narration before you correct students within the 10-second time limit. In reality, it will only take you 4 or 5 seconds to use behavioral narration, thus you will still have enough time to correct disruptive students.

So basically, after you give your directions, you will be doing nothing but monitoring the behavior of students. First you will narrate those students who follow your directions. Then within 10 seconds, you will correct students who still choose to be off task.

Calmly Restate Directions

When you observe students who are not following your directions, what do you say to them to get them back on task? Before we focus on what works, it is important to quickly look at what does not work. Do any of these responses sound familiar?

- *"Terrel, you're out of your seat. Why are you getting up when you should be working?"*

- *"Connie, how many times do I have to talk to you about your misbehavior? What am I going to do with you?"*

- *"Jack, I'm sick and tired of you bothering me. Enough is enough. When are you ever going to learn to behave like the other students?"*

These responses may sound familiar because they are examples of the most common behavior management procedure used by teachers today—it is called *nagging.* Nagging may make you feel a little better at the time, but it has a negative impact on your students. Students know that when you nag, you do not mean business (Jones, 2000), and your nagging sets a negative tone in your classroom.

When you are effective and mean business with students—be it on days when you are giving a standardized test or do not feel well, you likely do not nag the students to do what you want. When teachers mean business, they tell the misbehaving students exactly what they want them to do in a calm, matter-of-fact manner (Walker et al., 2004). Simply put, you will repeat to the student the directions they should follow and what consequence, if any, they have chosen to receive.

- *"Terrel, the direction was to stay in your seat when you are working. You have chosen to receive a warning."*

- *"Connie, you should be sitting and looking at me without talking. You have chosen to go to time out."*

- *"Jack, you need to do your own work without shouting out. This is the third time I have had to talk to you today so you have chosen to have me call your parents."*

Such direct communication of your expectations is the most effective way to let students know you are serious about making sure they stop their inappropriate behavior.

Provide Consequences From a Discipline Hierarchy

A discipline hierarchy is a list of consequences students will receive if they choose to be disruptive. Here are two examples:

Elementary

First disruption:	Warning
Second disruption:	5 minutes of time out
Third disruption:	10 minutes of time out
Fourth disruption:	Call to parents
Fifth disruption:	Send to principal's office
Severe clause:	Send to principal's office

Middle/Secondary

First disruption:	Warning
Second disruption:	Stay 1 minute after class
Third disruption:	Stay 2 minutes after class
Fourth disruption:	Call to parents
Fifth disruption:	Send to vice principal's office
Severe clause:	Send to vice principal's office

See chapter 40 on page 213 for details on how to develop a discipline hierarchy for your classroom.

Consequences Need to Be Provided to Students as a Choice

For a consequence to have the maximum impact on student behavior, it needs to be presented to the students as a choice (Canter & Canter, 2001a):

"I'm going to give you the directions I want you to follow to be successful in this classroom. If you choose to disrupt rather than follow the directions, you will choose to receive the appropriate consequence."

There is much more than semantics involved when you present consequences to students as a *choice.* By letting students know they will be *choosing* if they do or do not receive consequences, you are no longer the "bad guy" who is *giving* the students consequences. Your students choose their behavior and the consequences that follow:

- *"Kevin, you were talking instead of working. You have chosen to stay after class."*

- *"Jonathan, you were out of your seat bothering your classmates. You have chosen to have me call your parents."*

- *"Tony, hitting is not acceptable in this class. You are choosing to immediately go to the principal's office."*

When you provide consequences as a choice, you send a powerful message to all your students. The message is:

- *You* are accountable for your actions.

- *You* are responsible for what does and does not happen to you.

- *You* are in control of your success in this classroom.

Take Corrective Action Every Time Students Are Disruptive

Students will never believe you mean business and follow your directions until they know you will take corrective action—provide disciplinary consequences—each and every time they choose not to follow your directions (Sprick, Garrison, & Howard, 1998).

Being firm and providing corrective feedback is often a major struggle for many teachers. These characteristics are not consistent with their view of how they want to present themselves:

- *"I don't want to be hard-nosed like my teachers were when I was going to school."*

- *"I want to give my students the freedom to be who they are in my classroom."*

- *"I want my students to like me."*

Students need structure and limits. There is perhaps nothing more harmful we can do to students than allow them to disrupt or misbehave without showing them we care enough to let them know their behavior is not acceptable. Students need to learn that inappropriate behavior carries with it very real consequences. This is also true in the real world, and is an important life lesson to learn in the classroom.

Make Sure You Correct Inappropriate Talking

Never forget that inappropriate talking—such as students shouting out, talking when they should be working, or talking too loud—will likely be the number one problem you encounter. Why?

First, if you are like most teachers, inappropriate talking accounts for close to 80% of the disruptive behavior you encounter. Simply imagine how many times each day you have to stop what you are doing to "shh" students who are talking or tell them to "quiet down" or "stop interrupting" (Jones, 2000).

Equally important, inappropriate talking is what I call a *cornerstone* behavior. It is almost always the first disruptive behavior students choose to engage in to test whether or not you mean business. Students carefully watch to see how you respond when they talk out of turn or talk to their neighbors when they should be quietly working.

If students see that you do not take their talking seriously enough to respond in a meaningful manner, they will take this as a clear message that they can test you even further to determine how they can and cannot misbehave. Soon you will find students getting out of their seats when they should be in them, then trying to get out of working, and eventually engaging in more difficult behavior problems.

> You must understand that students do not suddenly become defiant, fight, throw tantrums, and so forth. By the time these misbehaviors occur, your students have tested you to see what they can and cannot get away with. This testing starts with inappropriate talking.

Until you can stop inappropriate student talking, you will be unable to establish a classroom environment in which students learn they cannot get away with doing what they want versus what you want. Everyone will lose in this circumstance.

Catch Students Being on Task

After you have provided consequences to students, find the first opportunity you can to narrate their on-task behavior. Be sure to show students that you are not simply going to limit their inappropriate behavior, but that you are equally committed to supporting their appropriate behavior as well. For example:

> *Jake is poking and talking to students sitting next to him on the rug. You correct his behavior. A few minutes later, you see he is behaving appropriately so you narrate his behavior by saying, "Jake is sitting on the rug with his hands to himself, paying attention and not talking."*

BE PREPARED FOR STUDENTS TO TEST YOU

When you take corrective action and set limits, most of your students will quickly stop their disruptive behavior. Your noncompliant students, however, may escalate their behavior to test your resolve (Walker et al., 2004). These students may try a number of behaviors, including pretending to comply or becoming upset.

Students Who Pretend to Comply

When you set limits with some students, they will appear to comply with your directions but are only *pretending* to do so, as shown in the following example:

> *You see two students talking instead of working. You correct the student behavior by saying, "Will and Nina, the directions were to work without talking. This is a warning." The students quickly pick up their pencils, place them on their assignment sheet, and appear to be working. As soon as they notice you are not paying attention to them, they immediately begin to talk again.*

Some students try to lull you into believing that they are doing what you have asked them to do by engaging in behaviors that look like they are complying when in fact they are not. If students learn that they can get away with pretending to do what you want, you can be sure they will continue to test you at every turn.

Move in. You need to let students know that your goal is not for them to *pretend* to be on task, but to *actually* be on task. This will require you to let students know that you are aware of their misbehavior and will not tolerate it. What will you want to do?

The most effective way to let students know you will not tolerate their continued testing is to *move in* on the disruptive students. Calmly walk up to the students and let them know you are aware of their behavior and expect them to comply with your directions (Canter & Canter, 2001a). For example:

> *You observe Will and Nina talking again. You walk up to their desks, and calmly tell them, "I cannot let you keep talking instead of working. You have chosen to*

miss free time. If you continue talking, I will call your parents. Now I want you to get to work and complete your assignment."

You will send a clear message to all of your students when you stop what you are doing and take the time to walk up to the misbehaving students, provide them with a consequence, and let them know another consequence will follow if they do not shape up: "I will not tolerate your pretending to comply."

Students Who Become Upset

Some students will test your limits in a much more direct, angry manner:

Raquel is at a center bothering other students. You correct her behavior by saying, "Raquel, the directions were to work independently at your center. This is the third time I have had to speak to you today. You have chosen to have your parents called."

Raquel angrily responds, "I didn't do anything. You're picking on me again."

You attempt to explain yourself by saying, "I'm not picking on you," but all she does is become more upset and argue her point by saying, "You are picking on me—you always do. I don't have to listen to you!"

Soon you are frustrated by the disruption Raquel's escalating outburst is causing to the classroom. You find yourself thinking you don't need to deal with this now: You need to stop her outburst. You say to her, "Okay, Raquel, just calm down, get to work, and I won't call your parents."

You have students who have learned that when teachers set limits on behavior all they need to do is become upset and make a scene in order to get their way. In fact, students know the more upset they get, the better it will be for them because they realize that most teachers would rather do almost anything else than deal with angry student outbursts. What do you do if you have such students?

Calmly stand your ground. Keep in mind some students are experts at "hooking" you with their anger. You can take several steps to avoid being manipulated by these students.

Stay calm. Students know how to respond when they see their teachers become upset with their angry outbursts: get even angrier. It takes two people to fight. Students will feed off your emotional upset and use it to further fuel their own anger. The best response to this is to remain calm. The more upset your students become, the calmer you need to be. Your calm manner will defuse student anger (MacKenzie, 1996).

Do not argue. Remember this rule of thumb: You will never win an argument with your students. Why? Students are experts at arguing with adults—you are not an expert at arguing with students. Do not ever get into an argument with students. Instead, stand your ground and simply keep repeating what you want them to do (Walker et al., 2004):

> *Raquel comes into your classroom. Instead of going to her desk and starting to work, she begins provoking students nearby. You calmly walk up to her and correct her behavior, saying, "Raquel, you are to go to your seat and get to work. This is the second time I have had to talk to you today so you have chosen to miss your free time."*

> *As usual, Raquel begins to become upset and argue with you: "I didn't do anything. Samuel was talking to me first!"*

> *Remaining calm, you simply keep repeating your directions: "Raquel, you are to go to your seat and get to work."*

> *As Raquel keeps trying to argue, you keep calmly repeating, "Raquel, you are to go to your seat and get to work." Recognizing that she cannot provoke you or engage you in an argument, Raquel finally sits down and gets to work.*

Move out. With older students, it may be useful to *move out* of the classroom to speak with them about their behavior (Canter & Canter, 2001a). When you move out of the classroom, you are removing the audience of the student's peers. That can prove to be very useful.

When you calmly stand your ground, you will demonstrate to students that you do mean business. You cannot stop students from becoming upset, but you can choose not to let their distress sidetrack your efforts to stop inappropriate behavior.

Have a Backup Plan

A small number of students will test you to the limit. They want to see what you will do if they refuse to stop their disruptive behavior:

> *Ian is loud and disruptive while you are trying to teach a lesson. You correct his behavior and tell him to go to the time-out area to calm down. Ian angrily states, "I'm not going. You can't make me."*

> *Again, you calmly tell him, "Ian, go to time out or you will choose to have your parents called."*

> *He angrily replies, "I don't care!"*

> *Finally, you tell him, "Ian, go to time out or you will have to go to the principal's office."*

> *He immediately yells out, "I'm not going and you can't make me!"*

When Students Test You, Work On Your Relationship With Them

Teachers do not generally like to be tested by noncompliant students. As a result, most teachers tend to pull away emotionally from students who are stressful to deal with. This is a major mistake! Consider what happens in the following situation:

A student is defiant and the teacher has to remove her from the room, resulting in the principal suspending her. When the students returns to school the next day, warns the student in a stern voice: I'm not going to put up with any more of your nonsense today!

This response is at odds with a fundamental reality of student behavior:

The more students honestly believe you have their best interest at heart, the less likely they will be to challenge your authority.

When students test you, they are sending up a "red flag" signaling that you need to immediately put some work into building a more positive relationship with them.

If a student is defiant and the student's trip to the principal's office results in a suspension, take the opportunity to call the student at home and reach out to show you care. Tell the student, "I don't like having to suspend you. What can we do to make tomorrow a more positive experience for you?"

See chapter 12, Building Trusting Relationships With Students, on page 87 for more suggestions.

What can you do in this situation? Most teachers would immediately try to take the student on by saying, "I told you to go to the office and you will go!" The reality, however, is that if a student does not want to leave your classroom, you are unlikely to get him or her to the principal's office without help.

You know that you cannot leave the rest of the students to physically remove a student from the classroom. The most important point for you to recognize is that students know that you cannot *force* them to go to the office. Therefore, standing toe-to-toe with students and demanding that they leave the classroom is no-win position.

You have to have a backup plan to ensure you can get support to remove students from your classroom when students are out of control (Charles, 1999). Without a plan, you will be reluctant to stand up to some students for fear that you will be unable to handle the situation if they get out of control.

Most teachers have a plan that involves notifying the principal or other administrator to come to the classroom and remove the disruptive student:

> *When Ian refuses to go to the principal's office, you calmly tell him, "You either go to the principal's office or he will come here and escort you to his office. It's your choice." Ian still refuses so you call the office and notify the principal that you need assistance in your classroom immediately.*

You may be wondering what happens if the principal or other backup support personnel cannot come at that moment. What do you do then? If this happens, all you need to do is to tell the student what is happening and what will happen if they still choose not to leave your classroom:

> *When you call the office and the principal is not available, you tell Ian, "Ian, the principal is not able to come and I can't remove you from the classroom now, so you have a choice: You either go to the principal's office immediately on your own, or choose to have me take you there in 15 minutes when lunch starts."*

Knowing how to deal with students who seriously test your authority is critical to being able to stand your ground and letting students know you have raised your bottom line and will not tolerate their disruptive behavior.

PULLING IT ALL TOGETHER: CORRECTIVE ACTIONS

The third step in the Behavior Management Cycle is to take corrective action. In order to effectively do this, you need to remember these guidelines and suggestions:

- Establish a discipline plan that is effective with all of your students.

- Always provide consequences every time students disrupt in order to motivate them to do what you want. Inconsistently responding to some students simply does not work.

- Make stopping inappropriate talking an important priority.

- Follow the guidelines for taking effective corrective action.

- Be prepared for students to test you when you do set limits.

In the previous chapters, you learned the three steps in the Behavior Management Cycle. The next chapter shows you how to use this method in various classroom activities.

Chapter 11

Using the Behavior Management Cycle

In this chapter we look at the use of the Behavior Management Cycle during two of the most common classroom situations in which teachers often have difficulty dealing with student behavior: transitions and instructional activities. The challenges of each situation are discussed below, along with case examples that show how you can use the steps of the Behavior Management Cycle to increase your effectiveness for motivating all of your students to follow your directions.

EFFECTIVELY HANDLING STUDENT BEHAVIOR DURING TRANSITIONS

Getting students to transition from one activity to another or into and out of the classroom can be a major challenge. Let us look at how you would use the steps of the Behavior Management Cycle to motivate students to follow your directions during a transition.

Your students are constantly disruptive during transitions. Much to your consternation, a number of your students—Kevin, Ricardo, Lester, and Cara—view transitions as an opportunity to do what they want to do. You find you spend too much valuable class time on transitions, especially coming and going from the classroom.

You decide the students need to stop being disruptive when they enter the classroom, so you stop the class one day before the students enter and tell them exactly how you expect them to enter the classroom and get on task. As you speak, you make eye contact with Kevin, Ricardo, Lester, and Cara to send them a clear message that you expect them to follow your directions along with the other students:

"I'm not comfortable with how this class has behaved when you come into our classroom. I've allowed too much disruptive behavior. I know all of you can quickly and quietly come into class and get right to work. So when I say GO, I want everyone to walk directly to their seat, sit down, and begin working on the problem on the board without any talking."

To make sure the students understand how you want them to enter the classroom, and ensure that some of the students who have trouble with transitions succeed, you pick Ricardo and Cara to model how you want students to enter the classroom:

> "I would like Ricardo and Cara to show us exactly how you are to enter the classroom."

As the students model appropriate behavior by following your directions, you narrate their behavior:

> "Ricardo and Cara are walking directly to their seats. They are sitting down and have started to work on the problem on the board. This is exactly what I want to see all of you do."

You then cue the rest of the class to enter and get on task:

> "Okay, when I say GO, I want all of you to follow the lead of Ricardo and Cara and go directly to your seat, sit down, and get to work without talking. I will be looking for students who are following my directions. Ready, GO!"

As the students enter, you demonstrate you are on top of their behavior by carefully monitoring them and by narrating the behavior of those who are complying with your directions:

> "Barb is walking to her seat without talking. Ian is in his seat. Kyle is in his seat and has already started on the problem on the board without talking."

As you continue monitoring the students entering and getting on task, you notice that Lester is talking and disruptive rather than working, so you immediately take corrective action:

> "Lester, the directions were to sit down and do the assignment without talking. You have chosen to receive a warning."

You record Lester's disruption on your record sheet on your clipboard. As the students continue working on the assignment, you continue to demonstrate you are on top of their behavior by periodically narrating the behavior of students who are on task—especially the ones you are concerned about:

> "Lisa and José are still working on their problem without talking. I see Ricardo, Cara, and Kevin are also working without talking."

After you correct Lester's behavior, he chooses to stay on task and do his work, so you immediately narrate his behavior:

> "I see Lester is working on his assignment and is not talking."

Analysis of the Scenario: Transitions

When you effectively use the steps of the Behavior Management Cycle, you clearly tell all the students exactly how you expect them to make the transition. You take preventive steps to ensure some students who have difficulty during transitions are successful by having them model how to follow the directions.

Because you do not assume students will simply follow your directions, you consistently monitor and narrate the behavior of those who are on task. You pay particular attention to those students who have had difficulty during transitions, and you make sure to give them positive recognition by narrating their behavior when they choose to be on task.

You immediately take corrective action with the students who do not follow your directions. Equally as important, you narrate these students' behavior when they choose to be on task.

Thus, through the use of clear directions, behavioral narration, and corrective actions, you can quickly and quietly have all of your students enter the classroom, sit at their desks, and get on task.

EFFECTIVELY HANDLING STUDENT BEHAVIOR DURING INSTRUCTIONAL ACTIVITIES

Getting and keeping students on task during instructional activities is critical to your success as a teacher. Let us look at how you would use the steps of the Behavior Management Cycle to motivate your students to follow your directions during an instructional activity.

Whenever you attempt to conduct a lesson and class discussion, several students—Jesse, Shawn, and Pam—do not pay attention and are disruptive no matter what you do. The disruptive behavior of these students tends to set off the rest of the class. You find it hard to complete a lesson because you spend so much time trying to maintain order.

To ensure students do what you want, before you start your lesson, you review the directions you expect the students to follow and let them know that you will be looking for students who are complying:

"We're going to continue our lesson from yesterday. When I'm speaking during today's lesson, I expect all of you to do the following:

- *Stay in your seat with your eyes on me.*

- *Have nothing in your hands but your paper and pencil.*

- *Raise your hand and be called upon before talking.*

"I will be looking for students who follow my directions. They will earn points for the class."

To check if the students understand your directions, and to cue those students who have been causing problems, you ask students to repeat your directions:

"I want to make sure all of you understand my directions. I want Jesse, Shawn, and Pam to each tell me one of the directions I expect everyone to follow."

As you start your lesson, you make it a priority to let the students know that you are on top of their behavior by consistently narrating the behavior of those students who are on task. You keep an eye on Jesse, Shawn, and Pam, and you make sure you narrate their behavior so they can earn points for their classmates when they are behaving:

"I see Jesse, Shawn and Pam are paying attention, have their eyes on me, and are not talking. They have earned a point for the class toward free time."

During the lesson, you notice Pam is trying to talk to the students next to her. To let her know you expect her to pay attention, you narrate the behavior of students sitting by her who are on task:

"Lucy and Evan have their eyes on me and are not talking. That is another point for the class."

Pam notices that you are aware of her off-task behavior and quickly begins to pay attention again. Noting this, you immediately narrate her behavior:

"I see Pam has her eyes on me, is paying attention, and is not talking. She has earned a point for the class."

As the lesson progresses, you want to have the students participate in a discussion. You let the students know exactly the directions for participating:

"I want to hear your views on what I have just presented, and I want to make sure all of you have a chance to speak. I will not allow students to shout out or interrupt as I have in the past. Here is what I expect you to do during our discussion:

- *Raise your hand and wait to be called upon before you speak.*

- *Look at the person who is speaking.*

- *Do not make negative comments about what a classmate says."*

As you start the discussion, you make sure to call on and narrate the behavior of students who are following directions by silently raising their hands to be called upon:

> *"I'm going to call on Kyle: He has his hand up and is waiting to be called upon without talking out. He also earns a point for following directions."*

During the classroom discussion, Pam and Shawn start talking and shouting out inappropriate answers. You calmly correct their behavior:

> *"Pam and Shawn, the directions were to raise your hand and wait to be called upon before you speak. You have both chosen to stay after class."*

Pam quiets down, but Shawn becomes upset and begins to test you by arguing, "I didn't shout out. I had my hand up. You're not fair." You stay calm and again you immediately correct his behavior:

> *"Shawn, you have a choice: Either stop arguing with me, or you will choose to have me call your parents."*

Shawn continues to test you by saying, "Go ahead, call my parents. I don't care, and they don't care either." You calmly look at Shawn and firmly state:

> *"Shawn, I can't let you act this way in class. You know how to behave in class. I'm going to call your parents, and now your choice is to either calm down and participate in the discussion like the other students, or to be sent to the principal's office."*

Shawn finally calms down and you continue the discussion, making sure to narrate students who are following your directions.

Analysis of the Scenario: Instructional Activities

You make sure that management of student behavior is your top priority during the lesson.

You do not assume that the students know how to behave. Instead, you give them explicit instruction about how they are to follow your directions, both when you are teaching and during the ensuing discussion.

You take preventive steps to ensure that students who have had trouble during instructional activities get on task by having them repeat back the directions after you give them.

You do not assume that students will be motivated to follow your directions, so you narrate the behavior of students who are on task, and you use a classwide reward system as an additional incentive. To increase the motivation for students who have had problems staying on task, you monitor their behavior and make sure their appropriate behavior earns points for their classmates.

You consistently correct the off-task, disruptive behavior of the students, and you stay calm and do not back down when tested by a student.

By using the Behavior Management Cycle, you are able to conduct a lesson and lead a class discussion with minimal disruption from the students.

PULLING IT ALL TOGETHER: THE BEHAVIOR MANAGEMENT CYCLE

When you consistently use the Behavior Management Cycle, you will show your students that establishing a disruption-free classroom environment where everyone can learn is a top priority of yours and that your bottom line for behavior has been raised for every student to ensure everyone succeeds.

As long as you have students who continue to disrupt your class or act in a way that is not in their best interest, you will need to continue to use the Behavior Management Cycle to:

- Communicate clearly to your students exactly what you expect them to do before each and every activity.

- Monitor student behavior of those who are getting and staying on task as soon as you have given your directions.

- Firmly and calmly take corrective action if students continue to be off task or are disruptive.

The consistent use of the strategies of the Behavior Management Cycle will greatly enhance your ability to motivate your students to choose to behave appropriately in the classroom. Another factor that is critical to motivating your students is to build positive trusting relationships with them. In the next part of the book you will be presented specific strategies that effective teachers use to accomplish this goal.

Part 5

Building Trusting Relationships

Chapter 12

Building Trusting Relationships With Students

You could easily make the case that the keystone for effective classroom management is the teacher's ability to establish positive relationships with all of the students. Ask teachers who are highly effective in motivating students to succeed and they will confirm this point, as does the research:

> Establishing positive relationships with students can reduce disruptive behavior by up to 50% (Marzano et al., 2003).
>
> A positive relationship with students reduces disruptive behavior at all grade levels (Marzano et al., 2003).

For various reasons that will be considered in this chapter, many teachers do not take the steps needed to establish trusting relationships with their students, especially those they consider noncompliant. Let us examine what it takes to build relationships that can help you motivate students to increase achievement and reduce disruptive behavior.

THE STUDENT "TRUST DEFICIT"

Today many teachers report a great deal of difficulty in building strong, trusting relationships with many of their students. I have found that a major factor for this problem is the misconceptions these teachers have regarding what it takes to establish a positive bond with each and every student.

Many teachers honestly believe that students will naturally believe that they, the teachers, have their students' best interests at heart. As a result of this point of view, most teachers believe the students will automatically trust them, and positive relationships will quickly develop. This perspective is valid for most students, but unfortunately not for many considered noncompliant.

Most students arrive in your classroom with a basic foundation of trusting in teachers. In all probability, these students have parents who have motivated them to behave and succeed in school. In addition, these students have generally had teachers respond to them in a caring, accepting, and supportive manner during their time in school.

Experience has taught these students—again, probably most of your students—that they can trust you because they have learned that teachers do basically have their best interests at heart. Because of this, you can easily build a relationship with them and motivate them to work and to achieve to their full potential.

Some of your students, though, due to their life experiences, have developed a completely different perception of teachers. These students have learned not to trust teachers—and that certainly includes you. Simply stated, these students have a serious "trust deficit" when it comes to their relationships with teachers: Consequently, many are noncompliant students.

Students who have a "trust deficit" often have parents who have also had negative school experiences. As a result, the parents may communicate through their words and actions their belief that teachers often do not have the best interests of students at heart. Due to their learned attitudes, these students have often had conflicted relationships with teachers. These students have often experienced teachers as angry, critical, and punitive.

The Consequences of Expecting All Students Will Trust You

If you are like most teachers, you will find there is a serious downside of mistakenly assuming that all of your students will naturally trust you and want to be compliant. Why is this so?

Basically, any relationship is a two-way street. The students have needs they want you to meet, and you have needs you want them to meet. As a teacher, you are aware of all that you *give* to students to help them be successful—your time, attention, knowledge, and more. Have you thought about what you need your students to give *you* in order for you to be successful?

> The bottom line is you cannot do your job until your students choose to give you their attention and cooperation.
>
> Try getting students in their seats and ready to learn if they *choose* not to listen to you.
>
> Try teaching a lesson if the students *choose* not to pay attention.

Never forget that the choices your students make every day about their behavior will directly impact your effectiveness as their teacher. You cannot overlook this fundamental truth regarding motivating student behavior:

> **The more the students trust you and believe you have their best interests at heart, the more likely they will be to listen to you and do what you want.**

If you simply assume that all the students have a high enough level of trust and will be naturally motivated to do what you ask, you will probably be very disappointed. Instead, you will have students who continually fight you and are disruptive and defiant. From their perspective, you are "the teacher," and they have learned that teachers are not on their side.

To begin reaching students who have a trust deficit, always keep in mind that this deficit influences all of their perceptions and actions. Given this underlying mistrust of teachers, it is foolish to expect that these students will be as motivated as their classmates to please you and be compliant in respecting your requests or demands.

Reaching the students whose deficit in trust affects how they perceive and relate to you will take concerted action on your part. The steps you take to build relationships with your compliant students will not be enough. You will have to convince these students that you are on their side, you are not like other teachers, and you will ensure they have a positive growth experience in your classroom.

OVERCOMING THE STUDENT TRUST DEFICIT

Why can some teachers build positive relationships with students who have a trust deficit when their peers are unsuccessful? Instead of answering this question with a discussion on the attributes of such teachers, I would like you to complete an activity that has been very insightful for other teachers.

> *I want you to return to your early school years—somewhere between kindergarten and twelfth grade—and think of the "best" teacher you ever had. He or she may have inspired you or may have made a real difference in your life.*
>
> *What was so very unique about how this teacher related to you that enabled him or her to have a profound impact on you?*

What qualities did you identify? Other teachers who have completed this activity have offered a number of qualities:

- *"She really cared about me as a person, not just as a student."*

- *"She was a real person—not just a teacher."*

- *"He was always encouraging me and giving me positive support."*

- *"He pushed me farther than I ever thought I could go."*

- *"She would not let me get away with anything that was not appropriate."*

- *"He went out of his way to help me."*

The qualities that these special teachers demonstrated are similar to the qualities exhibited by the most effective teachers. These qualities can be guideposts to how you can overcome any trust deficits your students have and then build empowering relationships with all of your students.

Teachers who build strong trusting relationships with all of their students exhibit qualities that can be described as six specific strategies:

1. Take charge of the classroom.

2. Get to know your students.

3. Provide positive attention.

4. Be real.

5. Reach out.

6. Find the time.

You will recognize some of these strategies from earlier chapters in this book. All of these strategies will help you build productive relationships with your students.

Take Charge of the Classroom

When most teachers think about building relationships with students, they tend to think about being nice—giving students positive attention and spending time with them. Although these things are critical to building positive relationships, and will be discussed later, an often unrecognized step must be taken first before teachers can build the foundation of a trusting teacher-student relationship.

The foundation of any teacher-student relationship is *respect*. To build trusting relationships with all of your students, your students must respect you. You will begin to earn this respect when you take charge of your classroom. Why? A fundamental need of students is to have teachers who care enough about them take the personal responsibility to do whatever it takes to ensure they learn to behave in a manner that is in their best interest and that does not hinder the learning of any of their peers (Brophy & Evertson, 1976).

How do teachers who "take charge" act? They are firm and fair, and they stand their ground in a manner that respects the dignity of each and every student (Canter & Canter, 1992). Take a moment to remember the special teacher you had. It is likely this person clearly said what he or she meant and meant what was said. This teacher was prepared to back up his or her words with actions to ensure all students behaved successfully.

The phrase "taking charge" does not mean—as some teachers believe it means—you have to control the students and make them "fear your wrath." When teachers respond in a hostile, angry manner, their students may behave for a while, but they will never win the respect and trust of the students.

On the other hand, students will not respect or ever learn to trust teachers who try to get students to like them. These teachers try to be friends with the students and do not stand up to students when they are disruptive or disrespectful.

When all is said and done, the following reality exists:

> Until you earn the respect of your students, your other efforts to build a trusting relationship will not bear fruit.

Unless the students respect you, they will not value your praise, positive attention, or extra efforts to reach out to them.

Get to Know Your Students

Effective teachers recognize that building trusting relationships with students means putting in the time and effort to get to know them (Smith, 2004). These teachers know that they are not just teaching reading, arithmetic, science, or Spanish to a class of 20–35 students. They are teaching 20–35 young people who bring their own personal issues with them into the classroom.

For many years effective teachers have used the questionnaire format to help them learn about their students (Canter & Canter, 1992). For older students, teachers develop a questionnaire students can complete at the beginning of the school year. For younger students, teachers will talk with the students.

Useful questions to ask students include:

- Who are the adults you live with?

- Do you have any brothers or sisters? How old are they?

- Who are your best friends?

- What do you like to do best at home?

- Do you have any favorite hobbies?

- What is your favorite video game?

- If you had one wish, what would it be?

- School would be better if . . .

- What did your teacher do last year that you liked best?

- What did your teacher do last year that you liked least?

Teachers who use the student questionnaire report that it enables them to gain a clearer picture of what their students like and dislike and any issues they may have.

Another tool teachers find useful with older students is to have them keep a personal journal. The information that you glean from the students can prove invaluable. Most teachers will also write brief comments in the journals on what they read. Such comments give you the opportunity to demonstrate your understanding and caring for the issues your students may face. If you ask your students to keep a journal, you will also want to identify clear rules for how journals are shared with you—you obviously want to be sensitive to the needs of your students

Provide Positive Attention

Students need teachers to consistently give them positive attention. Providing positive support is especially important in building relationships with noncompliant students. In general these students are used to getting little or no attention and support from teachers—and perhaps also from home. Teachers tend to ignore them when they behave appropriately and respond to them when they are disruptive (Kerman, Kimball, & Martin, 1980).

If you visit an effective teacher's classroom, you will be struck by what a positive tone has been set. These teachers make it their business to provide positive attention to all the students each and every day or period. They follow this rule of thumb:

> **Make three positive comments to students for each negative one that is made (Colvin & Lazar, 1997).**

The positive comments you make to students need to be genuine. Students, especially older ones, can read you like a book and pick up when you are insincere with the praise and positive comments you make.

To build your relationships with your students, make it a priority to look for and respond to the strengths of your students: what they do right versus only what they do wrong.

Be Real

The teachers who can connect with their students relate to them in an authentic manner. They believe it is important to be a "real" person with the students, and not to simply come across as the teacher. They do not try to be friends with the students, but they do make it their goal to be friendly (Charles, 2000). They know that the more students can relate to them as real people and not just teachers, the more likely students are to like and trust them.

Being real means letting the students get to know you. It does not mean sharing your personal problems, but it does mean letting them know about you as a person and not just a teacher. Here are several ways you can be real with your students:

Let the students get to know you. Teachers who are effective in building positive relationships let the students get to know them as a person and not simply as "the teacher" (Smith, 2004). The more students can relate to you, the more likely they are to like you.

You may simply want to introduce yourself to the students and share pertinent and appropriate details about your life. Some teachers find it useful to create a small bulletin board at the beginning of the year with pictures of important people and events in their lives. In addition, you may include information about your interests, hobbies, and other details about yourself the students may find interesting.

Share what is happening in your life. When appropriate, let the students know what is going on in your life: what you did over the weekend or on your vacation, what significant people in your life are doing. You do not need to give too much information, just enough to let students know you are like them and may enjoy some of the same things they do.

Admit your mistakes. There is nothing more real than admitting your mistakes. All too many teachers are afraid that if they admit they have "messed up," they will lose respect in the students' eyes. Nothing can be further from the truth.

Students are not blind. They see when you make a mistake or do not handle situations in the best manner. If you get upset and lose it, mess up a lesson, or treat students rudely in front of their peers, do not make excuses for your behavior; simply admit your mistake and apologize. Students respect teachers who are able to take responsibility for their actions and admit when they have been wrong.

Reach out. When you thought about that special teacher in your life, the odds are you recalled how that teacher made you feel special, how the teacher made an extra effort to let you know someone cared about you and your success. All students need to know you care. This is of particular importance to establish positive relationships with those students whose "deficit of trust" is a barrier.

There is a business concept that can be valuable as a guiding principle in reaching out to students who do not trust you: The key to winning over a customer and keeping them happy is to exceed their expectations, be it for service or quality.

> Most noncompliant students, due to past experiences, have very low expectations for how teachers will relate to them. They believe teachers do not care enough about them to go out of their way to help them be successful.

To win over students and keep them motivated, you must *exceed their expectations* for how they believe teachers will relate to them. You accomplish this through your words and actions.

Contact students before school begins. Students who have had negative school experiences often are not looking forward to the start of school. If you get your class lists and recognize the names of students who have had problems in the past, try the following strategy. Instead of fretting or worrying about the potential problems you may have with these students in the coming year, simply pick up the phone and call them, introduce yourself, and share your commitment to help them have a positive experience in your classroom:

> *"I'm going to be your teacher this year. I'm calling because I want you to know I'm looking forward to having you in my classroom, and I want to know what I can do to make this the best school year you have ever had."*

Students who have had negative school experiences do not expect to hear from their teacher before school begins. Many teachers discover that reaching out in this manner before students enter their classroom can begin their relationships with these students on a positive note.

Greet students at the door. Whenever possible, you should personally greet students when they enter the classroom—and this especially applies to those whose relationships you need to work on. Many teachers use the "4-H strategy" of greeting each student at the door by using one of four greetings (Mendler and Curwin, 1999):

1. "Hello."

2. "How are you?"

3. A handshake.

4. A high-five.

This is an especially effective way to connect in a positive and respectful manner with students who need to know you care about them and their success in the classroom.

Talk with students about non-academic topics. One of the most effective strategies you can use to reach out to students and demonstrate that you care is to spend time talking with them about their interests, concerns, and feelings (Good & Brophy, 2003). Students who have troubled relationships with teachers rarely if ever have had teachers who took the time to sit down and just be there for them. The more time you spend talking with students about non-academic topics, the higher the probability that you will build a trusting relationship with them.

Contact students after a difficult day. Students who do not trust teachers will often have days filled with upset and conflict. These times are hard on both the students and the teachers.

The last thing these students would expect is to hear from their teacher in a caring manner after a difficult day. You will continue building a positive relationship with these students when you go out of your way to make a quick phone call to them before the next school day begins:

Teacher: *"Carney, I'm concerned that you had such a rough day today."*

Student: *"It was bad because you sent me to the principal again."*

Teacher: *"I understand you're upset. Carney, I care about you and I can't let you act up and be disruptive. I want to know what we can do differently tomorrow so that it is a better day for you."*

Student: *"I don't know."*

Teacher: *"It seems you start misbehaving when you are doing work on your own."*

Student: *"I don't like the work. It's boring and sometimes I don't understand it."*

Teacher: *"Let's try this: If the work is boring or you don't understand it, instead of talking to the other students and getting out of your seat, turn over your 'Help Card.' I'll come right over to help you. I'd much rather help you than have to send you to the principal again. Will this help?"*

Student: *"I guess so."*

Teacher: *"So what are you going to do if you are bored and need help?"*

Student: *"I'll turn over my Help Card rather than mess around."*

Teacher: *"Sounds good. I'm sure tomorrow will be a better day. Have a good night."*

(For information on Help Cards, see page 140.)

Many effective teachers report that reaching out to students after a difficult day can have a positive effect in changing how these students perceive them and their intentions (Canter & Canter, 2001a).

Recognize absences. Students who feel teachers do not care often believe they are unnoticed in class. When students are absent, phone or email them to let them know they were missed, and you care about them and how they are doing (Mendler, 2001).

Attend the students' extracurricular events. Another way you can demonstrate your caring to students is to attend events they are participating in—sporting events, artistic performances, and other events outside of the classroom (Smith, 2004). The impact of your taking the time to watch your students participate in events can be dramatic. Can you imagine a student "getting in your face" after you have gone out of your way to attend his or her athletic or artistic performance?

Find the Time

Many educators do not believe they have the time to reach out to students using these strategies. They believe they need to invest as much time as possible into planning their lessons and curriculum since they are under so much pressure to raise student achievement. This is a serious misperception, however, because you cannot afford *not* to put in the time to build and sustain relationships.

Remember that students who like their teachers are much less likely to take up valuable class time engaging in disruptive behavior. Further, students who are generally unmotivated by school are much more likely to be motivated to learn if they respect you and feel you genuinely care about their success. Sometimes the best use of the time you invest in raising student achievement is to put some extra effort into demonstrating your care and concern for them.

PULLING IT ALL TOGETHER

Building trusting relationships is a critical factor in motivating all of your students to choose to be successful. Remember that some of your students will enter your classroom with a lack of trust in you. To build trust in these students, you will need to:

- Earn student respect by taking charge in the classroom.

- Get to know your students.

- Provide positive support for the students.

- Let the students get to know you.

- Reach out to the students.

- Find the time to show you care.

A key to building positive relationships with some students is to reach out and build trust with their parents. In the next chapter you will learn how to effectively build positive relationships with your students' parents.

Chapter 13

Building Trusting Relationships With Parents

Parents are obviously the most important people in a child's life. The parents' love, support, and approval are a fundamental need of each and every child. Since parents are number one in importance, they are also number one in their ability to influence and motivate their children to be successful in school.

To put this in perspective, think about your own school experience. If you were successful in school, answer these questions:

- Why did you behave in school?

- Why did you strive to succeed academically?

If you are like most individuals who were successful in school, your parents played a major role in motivating your academic efforts. The parents of your students possess the same potential!

The importance of parental support has been studied and validated for years by educational researchers. When parents are involved and support the teachers:

- Students are better behaved (Henderson & Mapp, 2002).

- Student academic performance improves (Epstein et al., 1997).

Given the importance of the parents' role in their children's success, it is a critical problem that so many teachers are having difficulty building positive and sustaining relationships with many parents (Metropolitan Life Insurance Company, 2005). For the past 10 years, teachers have stated that the lack of parental support is a critical problem (Gibs, 2005; Langdon, 1996). What can be done to turn this around?

If you have not had as much success as you would like in getting support from your students' parents, the answer to your dilemma can again be found in examining the expectations and practices of effective teachers. These teachers can build positive relationships and get support from parents—even from those parents who have been unresponsive or hostile to other teachers.

EXPECTATIONS THAT PROMOTE POSITIVE RELATIONSHIPS WITH PARENTS

Parental Support Is a Must

Over the last 30 years, there has been a pervasive myth in educational circles that competent teachers *should* be able to handle all of the behavior issues of their students on their own without having to engage the support of the parents (Canter & Canter, 1976, 2001a). Teachers have been led to believe that contacting parents to help with student behavior is a sign of weakness or indicates a lack of professional ability.

Do any of these statements sound familiar?

"I avoid calling parents when there is a behavior problem with the students."

"I'm afraid the parents will judge me in a negative way if I contact them about a problem."

"I get defensive about having to contact the parents for help."

If you answered yes to any of these statements, you probably accept this myth as truth. You need to be aware of this because if you believe there is something wrong with contacting parents—that you are not being a competent professional—that internal belief will be reflected in how you speak and act.

Learn from your peers who demonstrate an amazing ability to work with parents and reject this myth outright. These effective teachers recognize that there is no way that they can bring out the best in all of their students unless they enlist and receive the maximum support possible from the parents. The message to learn from your highly effective peers is unequivocal:

> Getting parents on your side is critical to your success with your students!

It is not a sign of weakness to reach out to parents for support to help motivate their children to behave appropriately or achieve their maximum potential. In fact, it is a sign of strength: a sign that you are committed to students learning to behave and achieve and that you will do whatever it takes to ensure this goal is reached. Who better to enlist in this effort than the most important and influential individuals in the children's lives?

Why are parents critical to your success? Why is the support of parents so vital to your ability to motivate all of your students to reach their potential? Parents can be powerful motivators and can reinforce and support your classroom management efforts.

Parents can be powerful motivators. No one can motivate the students like their parents. Parental support for their children's learning is as powerful tool as you can find to help students choose to behave and achieve (Henderson & Mapp, 2002). Parental approval is one of the most powerful motivators for students and can bring dramatic results when used effectively.

Many parents are not aware of how important their motivation can be, or how to use their influence to help their children. Through establishing a positive relationship with the parents of your students, you will be able to guide the parents toward using this influence to benefit you and the students.

Parents can reinforce and support your classroom management efforts. In reality, your options are limited when students choose to be disruptive. Corrective actions such as time out, detention, going to the principal, and so forth work for some of the students, but not all.

A small but significant number of noncompliant students may not care about any corrective action you take at school. The only way you will get the "attention" of these students is to involve their parents in actively supporting your classroom management efforts.

> Through their words and actions, you need the parents to send their children a clear, unequivocal message: *We will not tolerate your inappropriate disruptive behavior at school.*

Students must know that if they choose to misbehave at school, they will have to answer to you *and* their parents. When they disrupt, they will choose to receive corrective actions from you *and* their parents. For you to gain this level of support from some parents, you will need to take a number of steps to build a positive trusting relationship with them.

Reach Out to Parents

In the past, teachers could naturally count on receiving the support they needed from parents simply because of the esteem their profession commanded in the eyes of society. This is not necessarily true today. For countless reasons, today our profession does not command the unquestioned respect and support of many parents. Whether we like it or not, today you have to go out of your way to win many parents over if you want to have a positive, supportive relationship with them.

In order to get the support you need, you have to take the initiative and systematically reach out to many parents. You have to accept that there is a high probability that some of these parents have had negative school experiences. As a result, they may not have much trust or faith in the educational system in general. More importantly, they may not have much trust or faith in you as the teacher.

All too many of today's teachers still expect that they will simply be given the support they need and should not have to earn it. As a result, teachers who have this expectation do not feel they need to go out of their way to reach out and earn the trust of the parents.

Effective teachers recognize that they need to reach out and win over all the parents to get the support they want and need—particularly those parents who have negative perceptions of school and teachers.

STEPS FOR BUILDING POSITIVE RELATIONSHIPS WITH PARENTS

Effective teachers take the following steps to build supportive, trusting relationships with parents.

Contact Parents Before School Begins

Just as it can be helpful to contact your students before school begins, it can be helpful to contact their parents before the school year to begin the year on a positive note. Most of your students' parents will only need a simple note from you that introduces yourself and lets them know you are looking forward to working with their child (Jones, 2000).

For those children who have a record of difficulty at school, you may want to follow up on your note by calling the parents and the student about the upcoming school year (Sprick et al., 1998):

> *"I'm going to be Mika's teacher this year, and I wanted to talk with you about how we can work together to ensure this is the best school year he has ever had. I want to know what you think I can do to help your son be successful."*

Remember that parents of students who have difficulty at school are probably used to hearing from teachers only when there is a problem. Contacting them in a caring, positive manner before school begins will show them that you are there for their child.

Let Parents Know Your Classroom Management Plans

To gain parental support for your classroom management efforts, let them know how you will be handling their children's behavior (Wong & Wong, 1998). At the beginning of the school year, send parents a copy of your classroom rules (page 207), positive feedback strategies (page 210), and corrective actions (page 213).

Send Parents Positive News About Their Children

One of the most effective strategies to build positive relationships with parents is to make positive phone calls or send positive emails to them when their children have had a good day in class (Smith, 2004). Most communication from teachers to parents tends to focus on student problems. This creates a negative tone to the teacher-parent relationship. If you want to win over the parents, nothing will help you more than to balance the times you tell them about the problems by consistently telling them about the successes of their children.

As a simple rule of thumb, plan to make two positive contacts with parents each day through phone calls, notes, or emails. This will take only a few minutes and can prove to be invaluable in gaining the support of parents.

Make Home Visits

Many teachers find that going to their students' homes is a meaningful strategy for showing they care. Your taking the time to visit a student's home and meet with the parents demonstrates to both student and parents that you are not like the "other" teachers. Home visits can go a long way toward establishing a positive relationship with both the students and the parents. This can significantly help in ensuring the student will be successful in your classroom (Mendler & Curwin, 1999).

Be sure to determine what your district or school policy is on making home visits before you use this strategy. Some school districts may not allow teachers to make home visits alone.

Document Problems You Have With Students

If you need to contact parents about problems with their child, you must have an accurate record of the issues and how you have attempted to handle them. An excellent way to record this is to keep an incident sheet or card:

<u>Student Name</u>: Thad Heller

<u>Date</u>: 9/21/05   <u>Time</u>: 11:03   <u>Place</u>: Classroom

<u>Issue</u>: Thad was talking out during the math lesson. When I told him to stop, he talked back and refused to cooperate.

<u>Actions Taken</u>: Took corrective actions from the discipline plan. Took Thad aside and spoke with him.

You are much more likely to gain the parents' support if they know you have tried to handle the child's problems on your own before you contacted them.

COMMUNICATING EFFECTIVELY WITH PARENTS ABOUT STUDENT PROBLEMS

Speaking with parents about issues with their children can be stressful. What you say and how you say it will obviously either help or hinder your relationship with the parents. This is why it is very useful to write notes on what you are going to say whenever you speak with parents on the phone or face to face (Sprick et al., 1998). Here are points you will want to cover:

Begin By Letting Parents Know You Care About Their Child

When you contact parents about a problem their child is having, they will probably be upset, defensive, or both. You need to be aware of this natural response when you begin your conversation.

Rather than simply "unloading" about what the student has done wrong, clearly let the parents know that you have their child's best interest at heart:

> *"I want to talk with you because I care about Rafael and I'm concerned that his behavior in class is going to hinder his success in school."*

Do Not Make Subjective Comments: Be Objective When You Describe the Student's Behavior

Avoid making vague, subjective, or judgmental comments regarding the student:

> *"She has a bad attitude and is always in trouble."*

> *"He has an anger problem and doesn't get along with anyone."*

> *"He never stops talking and won't listen to anything I say."*

Such comments will set a negative tone and can make parents very defensive.

It is much more productive to explain in specific, observable, and nonjudgmental terms what the student did or did not do. If you meet face to face with the parents, you may want to present documentation to support your point:

> *"Here's the issue: During the past 4 days, Rafael has refused to do his work on five occasions. He simply keeps saying that the work is too hard or boring and that he does not have to do any work he does not feel like doing."*

Explain What You Have Tried to Do to Help the Student

Parents want to know that you have tried to help their child before you contact them. Let the parents know all the steps you have taken to help the student solve the problem:

"I sat down with Rafael and discussed the issue with him. I went over the assignments with him and determined that when I sit with him, he can do the work just fine—it is not too hard. I made him stay in and finish the work. In addition, I had him talk with the counselor and principal. We all feel it is in Rafael's best interest to involve you in our efforts to help him with this issue."

Ask Parents for Their Ideas on the Problem

No one knows the child as well as the parents. Ask them for their input on their child's issues. You may want to ask questions such as:

"Is this a problem your child has had in the past?"

"Do you have any idea why your child may be having this problem?"

"Is there something going on at home that could be affecting your child's behavior—a divorce, separation, illness, a move, or sibling issues?"

Discuss the Steps You Plan to Take to Further Help the Student

Let the parents know that you will continue working with their child to help him or her be more successful. Let the parents know the next steps you plan to take to help their child:

"I'm going to set up a system that Rafael can use to signal me if he is having trouble with an assignment, rather than becoming upset. I'm also going to let him know that he can earn points toward special privileges for every assignment he completes on his own without complaining."

Explain Why the Parents Need to Work With You to Solve the Problem

Some parents honestly do not understand how important their support is to helping their child be successful at school. Discuss with the parents how important it is that they work with you to help their child:

"I will do all that I can to help your child, but it is definitely in his best interest that he understand we are all working together to help him. He needs to know that you and I will not tolerate him putting in anything less than his best effort.

"I think it would help Rafael if we set up a system that has him complete at home any work that he does not finish at school. How does that plan sound to you?"

Express Confidence That the Problem Will Improve When You Work Together

Parents will be concerned or worried when there is a problem with their children. It is very useful to let them know that you are confident there is a solution available:

> *"I'm confident that Rafael's effort will improve if we work together. I've worked with many children like him and have found that their motivation dramatically improves when both the parents and the teacher send a clear message through our words and actions that we expect them to do their work."*

Let the Parents Know You Will Follow Up With Them

Make sure the parents know you will stay in touch with them regarding their child's progress. Give the parents a specific date when you will follow up with a call, note, or email:

> *"I'll call you in a week to discuss how Rafael is doing. I want you to feel free to contact me any time you feel the need to talk about his progress."*

PULLING IT ALL TOGETHER

Parents are the most important people in your students' lives. Their support is vital to helping you build positive relationships and motivate their children to be successful.

In order to build trusting relationships with parents, keep the following in mind:

- You must have parental support in order to reach some students.

- You will have to reach out to some parents to gain their trust. In order to do this you will want to take the following steps:

  * Contact parents before school begins.

  * Send parents your classroom management plan.

  * Share positive news with parents.

  * Make home visits.

  * Document your efforts.

  * Plan what you will say when you communicate with parents.

HOW TO BUILD TRUSTING RELATIONSHIPS WITH STUDENTS AND PARENTS THROUGHOUT THE YEAR

This overview will help you integrate steps toward building positive relationships with students and their parents throughout the year. Use this as a guide for your efforts as the school year progresses.

Before the School Year Begins

Begin building relationships with students by proactively reaching out to them and their parents before the school year begins:

____ Write introductory notes to all students and parents.

____ Call students who have had difficulties.

____ Call the parents of students who have had difficulties.

At the Beginning of the School Year

When the school year begins, you can continue building positive relationships with your students by getting to know them, having them get to know you, and—of utmost importance—earning their respect.

____ Take charge in the classroom.

____ Establish high expectations for behavior.

____ Provide positive attention.

____ Get to know your students.

____ Let the students get to know you.

____ Send parents a copy of your classroom management plan.

____ Begin making positive phone calls, sending positive notes to parents.

Throughout the Year

Maintain high expectations for behavior and continue providing positive attention. Reach out to all of the students and their parents. Make it a priority to put special effort into relationships with students who are having difficulty in class.

____ Spend time talking with students regarding non-academic topics.

____ Attend student extracurricular events.

____ Call students after a difficult day.

____ Call students when they are absent.

____ Celebrate student birthdays.

____ Continue positive communication with parents.

____ Conduct home visits.

Part 6

The 2-Week Turnaround Program

Chapter 14

The 2-Week Turnaround Program

What if you are reading this book *after* the school year has begun? How can you turn around students who are not behaving appropriately or up to your expectations? A turnaround in student behavior will not come in an instant, but it can be done over time. Most teachers report it takes at least 2 weeks of consistent effort to begin the process of re-teaching students how you expect them to behave. The program outlined in this chapter will give you the tools to make that happen in your classroom.

TURNAROUND PROGRAM GUIDELINES

The guidelines below will help you create a 2-week turnaround program.

Read Parts 1 through 5 of This Book

Before you go any further, make sure you have read all of the chapters in Parts 1–5 of this book. These chapters will give you the foundation and guidelines for establishing a class-room environment that promotes academic success.

Pinpoint the Activities in Which Misbehavior Constantly Occurs

In order to turn around the behavior in your classroom, you first need to determine those activities where disruptive behavior interferes with the learning process. For example, are you having problems during transitions, when students are at centers, or during teacher-directed lessons?

Use Diagnostic Worksheet 1: Pinpointing Problem Situations (page 116) to help you focus on the situations or activities in which you are having trouble. Check all items that apply.

Determine the Problems You Need to Turn Around in Each Activity

For each activity or situation you identify as problematic, fill out Diagnostic Worksheet 2: Specifying Problem Behavior (page 117). This will help you organize your thoughts and conduct your lesson in the most effective manner.

Review the corresponding chapters in Parts 7–9. You will be using the content in the chapter as a guide to teach your students your exact behavioral expectations for this situation. Make changes or additions based on your own circumstances.

WHAT TO DO BEFORE YOU BEGIN THE TURNAROUND PROGRAM

Assess Your Rules, Corrective Actions, and Positive Feedback Policies

Before you begin your turnaround program, assess your rules, corrective actions, and positive feedback policies. When student behavior is a problem, it is always a good idea to review your classroom rules, corrective action hierarchy, and positive feedback strategies. You may need to make changes in the policies and the way you implement them. Ask yourself the following questions:

- **Do I need to change the classroom rules to address student misbehavior?** For example, if swearing and teasing are a problem, then "No swearing or teasing" should be one of your classroom rules that is in effect at all times during the day and subject to corrective actions if broken.

- **Are the corrective actions appropriate? Do they need to change?** Corrective actions do not have to be harsh, but they do have to be something students do not like. Even more importantly, they must be used consistently to be effective, and you need to feel comfortable implementing them.

- **Are my positive feedback strategies effective? Do I need additional ways to provide behavioral narration?** To be effective, positive feedback needs to be fresh, motivating, and sincere. It also needs to be given frequently and to all students whenever possible.

Review the policies lessons on classroom rules (page 207), corrective actions (page 213), and positive feedback (page 210) for guidelines on making changes. You can also use a copy of the worksheet on page 115 to record your ideas for new rules, corrective actions, and positive feedback.

Develop a Classwide Reward System

It is highly recommended that you plan a classwide positive feedback system, or reward system, to help motivate your students to turn around their behavior. When students have been misbehaving in a classroom, they may need strong incentives to change their behavior patterns. A classwide positive feedback system can provide this incentive. See the policies chapter on positive feedback (page 210) for guidelines on setting up such a system.

Tell Students You Will Be Raising Your Expectations for How They Are to Behave

When you begin a turnaround program, have a discussion with your students about how you will be changing or raising your expectations for their behavior. Emphasize that you will be teaching them how you expect them to behave from that day on. Make it clear that you will no longer allow students to engage in behavior that stops you from teaching, that keeps other students from learning, or that is not in their own best interests.

As the teacher—the individual in charge of the classroom—it is important that when you have this discussion with your students, *you* take responsibility for the problems that are occurring in the classroom.

Too often, the tendency is to blame the students:

"I've had it with too many students in this room acting up, disrupting, and not listening to me! You all need to shape up, and from now on you are going to shape up. If you don't, I'm going to do whatever it takes to let you know you can't get away with messing up in my classroom."

Blaming students will not motivate them to learn to behave in an appropriate manner. All it will do is create a negative confrontational relationship between you and them. Instead, let students know that you expect change in the classroom and, most importantly, that you are going to be the agent of change.

Tell them you want all of them to be successful, and you are going to create the best environment for learning:

"I want to talk to all of you about the misbehavior that has been going on in this room. I do not feel I have done an effective enough job teaching you how to behave in this classroom. How do I know? Too many of you do not listen to me, talk when you need to be quiet, disrupt when you need to work, or make fun of your classmates. This needs to stop.

"From this moment forward, I will not allow any student to break a class rule or ignore the directions I give. I will use corrective actions every time you choose to misbehave. In addition, I will give you much more positive feedback when your actions show me that you are following my directions. I want all of you to know I recognize your positive behavior, not just your misbehavior.

"I know I have made speeches like this before. This time I am committed to making a change. I will teach you how to behave. I will conduct lessons on the appropriate behavior that I expect from all of you throughout the day.

"I know all of you can behave, and I will do everything I can to make sure you do. I'm responsible for creating a classroom in which you can learn to the best of your ability, free from disruptive behavior. I will make sure you have that kind of environment from this day forward."

Such a statement will help prepare students for the lessons you will teach on behavior and the changes that will take place in how you respond to their behavior.

Discuss Changes in Your Policies Related to Rules, Corrective Actions, and Positive Feedback

Let the students know if you plan to make any changes in your rules, corrective actions, and positive feedback. Many teachers find such changes are necessary. It is important that you communicate these changes to the students at the very beginning of your turnaround efforts. Do not surprise your students with a new plan of action.

CONSISTENCY IS THE KEY

The key to turning around behavior is to consistently follow the guidelines for teaching behavior. As stated, the foundation for teaching behavior is based on giving the students effective directions for how they are to behave at all times in the classroom, providing positive feedback when they follow the directions and taking corrective action when they do not.

Some students will test your new expectations. That is to be expected. No matter what the students say or do, you need to consistently maintain your new expectations. It is up to you to help your students learn how to behave in a manner that creates a positive learning environment.

WORKSHEET FOR RULES, CORRECTIVE ACTIONS, AND POSITIVE FEEDBACK

New Rules

_____
_____
_____
_____
_____
_____
_____
_____

New Corrective Actions

_____
_____
_____
_____
_____
_____
_____
_____
_____

New Positive Feedback

_____
_____
_____
_____
_____
_____
_____
_____
_____
_____

TWO-WEEK TURNAROUND PROGRAM

Diagnostic Worksheet 1
Pinpointing Problem Situations

Instructional Settings Lessons

❏ Teacher-Directed Instruction
❏ Whole-Class Discussion
❏ Sitting on the Rug
❏ Independent Work
❏ Working With a Partner
❏ Teacher Works With a Small Group While Other Students Work Independently
❏ Working in Groups
❏ Working at Centers

Other Situations

_____

_____

_____

_____

_____

Procedures Lessons

❏ Attention-Getting Signal
❏ In-Seat Transitions
❏ Out-of-Seat Transitions
❏ Lining Up to Leave the Classroom
❏ Walking in Line
❏ Entering the Classroom After Recess or Lunch
❏ Students Going to Pull-Out Programs
❏ Distributing and Collecting Materials or Papers
❏ Attending an Assembly
❏ Emergency Drills

❏ Beginning of the Day or Period Routine
❏ End of the Day or Period Routine

Other Situations

_____

_____

_____

_____

_____

Policies Lessons

❏ Classroom Rules
❏ Positive Feedback
❏ Corrective Actions
❏ Bringing Appropriate Materials to Class
❏ Making Up Missed Work Due to Absence
❏ Sharpening Pencils
❏ Using Materials on Bookshelves or in Cabinets
❏ Individual Students Leaving Class to Go to the Restroom
❏ Late or Missing Assignments
❏ Student Helpers
❏ Taking Care of Desks, Tables, and Chairs
❏ Using the Drinking Fountain

Other Situations

_____

_____

_____

_____

_____

Classroom Management for Academic Success © 2006 by Solution Tree
www.solution-tree.com

TWO-WEEK TURNAROUND PROGRAM

Diagnostic Worksheet 2
Specifying Problem Behavior

Activity or Situation: _____

What specific problems are you having? (For example: Too much talking. Students do not follow directions. Students are not listening.)

_____

_____

_____

_____

_____

_____

Who is involved in the problem behavior?

❏ One student _____

❏ Two students _____

❏ A group of students_____

_____

❏ Most of the class _____

_____

❏ Other _____

_____

Part 7

Managing Instructional Activities to Promote Academic Success

Chapter 15

Introduction to Instructional Activities

INTRODUCTION

Instructional activities help to engage students during the learning process. To increase the academic achievement of students, you need to be able to quickly get the students on task and keep them engaged throughout the instructional activity.

OVERVIEW OF CONTENT FOR EACH INSTRUCTIONAL ACTIVITY

The chapter on each instructional activity will use the following format to ensure your ability to apply the concepts presented:

Introduction

The basic goals of each instructional activity and the most common behavioral problems that teachers encounter are briefly discussed before moving into the detailed chapter content.

Behaviors to Teach

As was discussed in chapter 1, research indicates that effective educators teach their students how they are expected to behave in each class activity at the beginning of the year. For each instructional activity you will be provided a list of behaviors most teachers find their students need to be taught to successfully engage in the activity.

Preventive Management Strategies

The goal of any classroom management program is to prevent problems from developing and/or minimize their disruptiveness to the classroom. In each chapter on an instructional activity you will be provided specific strategies to assist you in keeping students on task rather than being disruptive, and strategies that will enable you to quickly stop any disruptive behavior before it gets out of hand.

Best Practices for Instructional Strategies

Many behavior problems during instructional activities can be attributed to shortcomings in the instruction itself. For each instructional activity you will be provided examples of effective instructional strategies that will increase student motivation and engagement. These strategies are based upon both reviewing the available literature and the observations of effective teachers.

Moving Toward Self-Management

Another goal of an effective classroom management program is that it is designed to ensure students learn to manage their own behavior. Thus, for instructional activities where it is appropriate, you will be provided suggestions for how students can learn to take responsibility for increasing their own self-management.

Dilemma: Do You Teach Content or Manage Behavior?

During instructional activities what needs to be your top priority—making sure you teach content or manage student behavior?

If you are like the vast majority of educators, you will answer, "Teach content." This answer may seem logical given the pressures to cover the curriculum and raise achievement.

Here is the *reality* of the situation: You will never be able to conduct instruction and effectively teach your class until you are able to manage the behavior of *all* of your students.

All it takes to interrupt any lesson you are trying to teach is one student "talking out," one student noisily wandering around the classroom disrupting classmates who are working, or one student openly defying you.

The Consequence of Putting Content Before Behavior Management

It is a law of human nature that whatever is important to you receives the most attention from you. If you believe teaching content is more important to your success than managing student behavior, that belief will have several critical consequences that will affect your success.

First, the results will be obvious if you put content ahead of behavior when preparing for what you will do in the classroom. You will spend hours on your lesson plans and little or no time on determining how you will manage student behavior, especially the noncompliant ones, during the lesson. The consequence will likely be that you are not prepared for behavioral issues that can and will arise.

Second, of even greater significance is what takes place in the classroom. Whether you are aware of it or not, throughout the school day you constantly face a dilemma regarding what will get your attention—teaching content or managing behavior. For example:

You are in the front of the class teaching a new concept to the students when you notice that students in the back of the room are talking and not paying attention. You are torn: Do you interrupt your lesson before making your point to deal with their behavior, or do you continue your instruction? You think to yourself, "I'm here to teach. If students don't want to learn, that's their choice. I'll teach those who are interested." You half-heartedly try to "shh" the off-task students, then quickly continue the lesson.

Though the decisions you make to put teaching content before management seem well intended, they often result in unexpectedly negative outcomes. Do not forget that *students are always aware of what you are doing and what is important to you.* Students quickly learn that when you are busy teaching, you do not want to be distracted by dealing with behavior problems. Thus, when they see you fully occupied with your instruction, they will feel they have the license to do what they want. The results are often not good!

When other students notice that you are so intent on finishing your lesson that you permit the students in the back to talk, more and more of them either begin talking or become distracted by the commotion their peers are making. As the noise level grows, so does your frustration, and you end up spending the remaining time trying to get the students to be quiet and back on task.

No one becomes a teacher because they relish the thought of dealing with the disruptive behavior of students. The reality is, however, if you want to maximize the time available for instruction, you need to make it your priority to be sure all the students know how they are expected to behave, and you need to monitor their behavior to ensure that they get and stay on task. It helps to always keep this thought in mind:

> The unintended consequence of putting the teaching of content before management is that you spend more time and energy on management and less time actually teaching.

Chapter 16

Teacher-Directed Instruction

INTRODUCTION

The foundation of teaching is the ability to get and maintain the attention of students while you conduct instruction. This is often easier said than done. All too often, teachers have trouble getting the attention of all of their students when they start the lesson, keeping their attention as the lesson progresses, or both.

BEHAVIORS TO TEACH

During a teacher-directed lesson, students are expected to:

- Follow directions.
- Keep their eyes on the teacher.
- Stay in their seats.
- Do this without talking.

PREVENTIVE MANAGEMENT STRATEGIES

Remember: Management Before Instruction

The first time you conduct a teacher-directed lesson, do not worry about the students learning the content—make sure all students are paying attention and not disrupting. Never become so lost in teaching the lesson that you forget about monitoring student behavior.

Do Not Wait for Students to Be Quiet

Waiting for students to be quiet wastes time. Use your "attention-getting signal" (page 161) to make sure you have the attention of all students before starting the lesson. Be sure to immediately narrate students who are paying attention: "Juan has his eyes on me and is not talking." When needed, immediately take corrective action with students who are not following directions.

Use Behavioral Narration Throughout Your Lesson

Every minute or two during your lesson, look for students who are paying attention and are engaged in the lesson, and narrate their behavior. If students start to get off task, immediately look for on-task students who are sitting near them and narrate their behavior. This can cue the off-task students to get back on task.

Do Not Constantly "Shh" Students

Remember inappropriate talking is your number one problem. If using behavioral narration does not motivate students to stop talking, do not keep saying "shh"—take corrective action.

Make Your Corrective Actions as Non-Disruptive as Possible

If you need to take corrective action, do so in a manner that is as unobtrusive as possible to your lesson. If possible, walk up to the students while you are teaching and privately tell the students what they are to be doing—"The directions are to pay attention to me and not talk"—or tell them the consequence they have chosen. If you cannot get close to the students, simply tell them the directions they are to follow or the consequence they have chosen and immediately get back to the lesson.

Use the Power of Physical Proximity to Keep Students on Task

The closer you are to students, the less likely they are to misbehave. Seat students who tend to disrupt close to where you will spend the majority of your time teaching. When possible, move around the room as you teach and place yourself close to students who are distracted.

Stay *Withit*

Stay *withit* at all times. "Withit" is a term used to describe a teacher who is aware of and on top of student behavior. This is especially important if you are writing on the board. Never turn your back to your students when you are writing, but instead turn your body to the side and frequently look back to monitor the students.

Do Not Let Talking Get Out of Hand

If for any reason during the lesson more than five students are talking or not paying attention, use your attention-getting signal to get everyone's attention before continuing the lesson (see pages 161 and 162 for details on using an attention-getting signal).

Keep Students Actively Engaged

One of the most effective ways to prevent disruptive behavior is to make sure the students stay actively engaged throughout your lesson. Boredom leads to disruptive behavior. Make sure you never lecture more than 7–8 minutes without using some form of engagement strategy to involve all the students in the lesson. See part 7 beginning on page 119 for more ideas.

BEST PRACTICES FOR INSTRUCTIONAL STRATEGIES

Use Effective Presentation Skills

How you speak is as important as what you say. Effective presentation skills can help maintain student attention and keep them engaged in the lesson (Heim, 2001). Keep these useful tips in mind when speaking to your students:

- **Facial expression.** A *stone face* is a facial expression so bland that the message to students is cold and serious. An *open face* communicates enthusiasm and invites youngsters to pay attention and, when appropriate, to participate. Remember, it is okay to have fun, to care about whether students are learning, and to be a terrific teacher.

- **Gestures.** The most effective gestures are the ones you naturally use, but slightly exaggerated when directed toward a whole class. Hand movements actually re-energize you and invite student focus. More problematic for learners are gestures called *adapters*. These are the ineffective gestures you may make when you are extra nervous or distracted. Scratching, jiggling pocket change, twirling a pencil, twisting hair, or bouncing from one foot to the other are distracting and make it harder for students to focus on the lesson. You expect students to be still and not fidget, so it is important that you minimize fidgeting as well.

- **Eye contact.** Eye contact is one of your most valuable resources. Scan the whole classroom and students will believe you are "all seeing." Anytime you hold a student's gaze for a few seconds, you are making contact without the need for words. Depending on what your eyes "say," that contact can communicate anything from "Get back to work" to "I understand."

- **Voice.** Your voice brings emotion to life. Vary your pace, volume, and pitch. Project to the whole room, but pull students to the edge of their seats with a well-timed whisper. Most importantly, avoid yelling at students. It is a poor use of both your voice and your behavioral repertoire. When you need to be serious, use a firm, deliberate tone.

Use Engagement Activities

Use engagement activities to keep students involved. The more you engage students in the lesson, the easier it is to keep their attention and reduce disruptive behavior. As a general rule, you can expect students to listen to you for only about 7–8 minutes (depending upon their age) before you need to break up the lecture with an engagement activity (Rogers, 2001). An engagement activity involves the students in the learning process. Here are some strategies to use:

- **Choral response.** Having students vocalize is a terrific way to engage them, reinforce learning, and legitimize talking. One of the easiest techniques is a class choral (or physical) response, often to a specific or closed question, such as, "How many days are in this month?" You are looking for the one right response, almost as though you were asking a fill-in-the-blank question.

  Use the pacing and pausing of your voice to prompt students to fill in the void: "The song we just learned was called 'Head, Shoulders, Knees and _____ [Toes].'"

  Be alert. Just because you ask all students to answer does not mean that everyone knows the answer or that all voices will chime in. When the learning is important, have sections of the room repeat the answer and then invite the whole group to respond: "Nouns represent (*point to one row of students*) _____, _____, and _____ [persons, places, and things]. Okay, now everybody respond. Nouns represent _____, _____, and _____."

- **Stop and jot.** Have students listen carefully without taking notes. After a short time, stop and give them several minutes to recall the "chunked" information from your presentation. Shape the notes with them by guiding them through key points. This reconstruction of learning helps with mastering both facts and concepts.

- **Think, pair, share (or write, pair, share).** Between chunks of lecture, have students stop and think (or write). Then, divide the class into pairs and have students share with partners what they heard. Their task could be to define, restate points or procedures, describe, reflect, predict, justify, generalize, or create. Make the task short and simple and give students just a minute or two for discussion. Structure the sharing time so that each student in the pair participates. With more experience, pairs can correct each other, reach agreement, or provide supporting evidence.

- **Survey, voting, opinion polls.** Before peer pressure gets in the way, students are often happy to take an independent stand on an issue. When you make a presentation, stop and ask what they think might happen next in the story, which column is the correct one for borrowing, or how many servings of vegetables should be eaten each day. In the beginning, give students two or three clear choices. The intent is not to mix them up, but to check for understanding.

If it helps, collect their answers by secret ballot. Have the students close their eyes or put their heads on their desks and vote, giving a thumbs-up if they agree or a thumbs-down if they disagree.

You can even propose a value-added option: "Hand high if you are totally sure, halfway up if you are pretty sure, and just a wrist flip if it's your best guess."

Chapter 17

Whole-Class Discussion

INTRODUCTION

Whole-class discussions can be one of the most valuable instructional strategies in your teaching repertoire. To be successful, however, students must learn to participate appropriately: to listen to one another's comments, take turns speaking, and respect others' opinions. Your instructional plans can quickly fall apart when students blurt out answers, monopolize the conversation, avoid participating, ask irrelevant questions, or give inappropriate answers. Learning self-control, taking turns, and respecting others allow all students an equal opportunity to contribute to the discussion.

> ## BEHAVIORS TO TEACH
> During a whole-class discussion, students are expected to:
> - Raise their hand and wait to be called on before speaking.
> - Look at the student who is speaking.
> - Stay seated.

PREVENTIVE MANAGEMENT STRATEGIES

Make Your First Priority Teaching Students to Behave During Discussions

Students will never learn how to have a discussion where everyone is heard without students shouting out answers unless you teach them how to do it. Remember your first priority during any discussion is that the students engage in the appropriate behavior needed so that the discussion can be productive for all.

Only Call on Students Who Quietly Raise Their Hands

Do not call on students who are shouting out answers—this will only encourage them to continue. Recognize students who are quietly raising their hands to answer and narrate their behavior: "Terrell has his hand up and is not talking. I'll call on him."

Take Corrective Action if Students Continue to Shout Out Answers

If students continue to shout out answers, even with their hands up, you will need to take corrective action. Simply restate directions—"The directions were to raise your hands and wait to be called upon before speaking—that's a warning."—or provide the appropriate consequence.

Have Potentially Disruptive Students Model How to Behave

When you are about to begin a discussion, you may have several of the students who typically create problems during discussions model appropriate behavior. Simply doing this is a quick reminder to these students of how you expect them to behave.

Use Physical Proximity to Keep Students Engaged

Stand next to students who are having trouble participating appropriately during a discussion. Keep moving around the room and use your physical presence as a preventive tool. If you use a circle for your class discussion, have the disruptive students sit by you.

Have Students Clear Their Desks Before the Discussion

Have students clear their desks of any distracting objects before attempting a whole-class discussion. The fewer distractions, the easier it will be to keep all students engaged.

Have Students Pair Off When They All Want to Speak

When the entire class is eager to speak, pair students off and allow 1 to 2 minutes for each pair to share their opinions. Give them a 30-second wind-down warning before returning to the whole-class discussion.

BEST PRACTICES FOR INSTRUCTIONAL STRATEGIES

Keep All Students Engaged in the Discussion

Too often teachers consistently call on the first, second, or third hand up, or the same group of students (Good & Brophy, 2003). Here are some ideas for making sure everyone has an equal opportunity to speak and all students are engaged:

- Put students' names on craft sticks and place the sticks in a cup. Pull out a stick to determine who goes next. Call the name only after you have asked the question and provided some time for thinking.

- Give everyone two or three chips, tokens, or coins to spend by speaking during a lesson. Some students will be challenged to speak and spend their chips. Others will—perhaps for the first time—hold back their words and chips and select a better time.

- Have the seating chart in front of you with everyone's name on it. Make a tally mark on your chart when a student contributes to the discussion. This is a great way to monitor students who are actively participating, and note those who are too shy or reluctant and may have been overlooked. Eventually, you may decide to give a discussion grade based on participation, and this chart will help you decide that grade.

- Avoid calling on the first student to raise his or her hand. Wait for a number of students to signal their interest in answering before calling on one. You might even tell the class that you will wait until everyone has an idea. If after a reasonable amount of time some are not ready to participate, have them check in with a neighbor to see if they agree on an answer to the question.

Use "Think" or "Wait" Time

Many teachers quickly toss out questions and hastily reach for answers. This rapid interaction pattern diminishes thinking and learning (Rowe, 1986). After posing a question, allow at least 5 seconds for students to process it and formulate an answer (Good & Brophy, 2003). This kind of think time says to a student, "This question is interesting, and your response is worth the wait." The end result is better answers by more students, more often. Second-language learners and reluctant participants benefit from this change of pace. The students with the fastest hands in the class also learn to slow down and think before they speak.

Use Higher-Level Questions

Often teachers ask questions that do not stimulate students to use higher-level thinking skills. Develop a repertoire of questions that stimulate students to go beyond thinking on a surface level. Have students formulate answers, not just give responses. Ask questions that cause students to build, combine, synthesize, and extend their learning (Rogers, 2001). Ask questions such as:

- "What do you think?"

- "How does this relate to what we already know?"

- "How is that different?"
- "Why do you think this might be?"

MOVING TOWARD SELF-MANAGEMENT

Let Students Speak Without Raising Hands

For older students who have mastered discussion strategies, try having students simply speak one at a time without raising their hands or your calling on them.

Let Students Run the Discussion

Assign a student helper to facilitate or run the group while you become part of the class.

Chapter 18

Sitting on the Rug

INTRODUCTION

Sitting on the rug can create an intimate instructional environment in which to read a story or conduct a discussion with younger students. However, the closer children physically are to one another, the tougher it is to share the space without fidgeting and touching. Close quarters can quickly lead to other disengaging or off-task behaviors. However, it is possible and worthwhile for children to sit in close proximity and enjoy learning.

BEHAVIORS TO TEACH

This lesson has been divided or "chunked" into three parts. It is suggested that you teach the first part, then model it and check for understanding before moving on to the next part. Younger students will benefit from this step-by-step approach.

1. Preparing to Move to the Rug

When getting ready to go to the rug, students will:

- Stand up quietly and push in their chairs.
- Stand behind their chairs and wait to be told to come to the rug.
- Do this without talking.

2. Transitioning to the Rug

When transitioning to the rug, students will:

- Walk to the rug.
- Sit in their own spaces.
- Keep hands and feet to themselves.
- Remain silent.

(continued)

> ## BEHAVIORS TO TEACH (continued)
>
> ## 3. On the Rug
>
> When participating in a lesson on the rug, students will:
>
> - Look at the teacher or whoever is talking.
> - Raise their hands and wait to be called on before speaking.
> - Sit cross-legged with hands in lap.
> - Follow directions.

PREVENTIVE MANAGEMENT STRATEGIES

Teach Behavior First

Disruptive behavior can quickly result when children are in such close quarters on the rug. For the first few times you bring the students to the rug, do not be as concerned about the lesson as making sure the students learn how to sit and pay attention.

Do not allow yourself to ever be so lost in the lesson that you stop attending to how the students are following directions. For example, if you are reading a story to the students, stop often to monitor and give feedback to the students: "Kelly is paying attention to the story and staying in her space. William is keeping his hands and feet in his own space and is quietly paying attention."

Assign Seating

At the beginning of the year, some teachers assign each student to a spot and code that spot with an icon or a name so students know where to sit—like a seating chart. Assigning spots helps students be successful by making sure that you do not have students who are potentially disruptive sitting by one another. It also makes transitions quicker because students will not have to figure out where to sit, and there will not be any arguing about the "best spot."

Students may also have their own carpet square and learn the rule to keep all body parts inside their square. Masking tape can create a checkerboard on a larger carpet for a similar structure.

Be sure to place near you those students who have trouble sitting still.

If some students have great difficulty sitting still, try having them sit slightly away from other students so that their movement is not distracting. Make sure these students are not all placed next to each other for it may lead to more distracting behavior.

Establish Personal Space on the Rug

When confined to desks and chairs, students have a clear sense of their personal space or "territory" and know when they are encroaching on the space of others. When on the rug, however, students may not know exactly how much space is theirs and consequently may bump or lean on other students inadvertently.

Help students gain a sense of personal space by asking them to sit "a hand's distance" apart. That is, when seated on the rug, have students place their hands on the floor on either side of them with fingers pointing outward. As students place their hands adjacent to their neighbor's, fingertips to fingertips, they can easily see the boundaries of their own personal space.

Keep Students Actively Engaged

Again, the more you actively engage students in the lesson, the less disruptive their behavior will be. Every few minutes, make sure you have the students do something that will keep them actively engaged.

Let Students Get Up and Move Around

If the lesson is running long, do not expect the students—especially those who are quite young—to sit quietly on the rug. Break up the lesson with some quick physical activity such as stretching or dancing.

BEST PRACTICES FOR INSTRUCTIONAL STRATEGIES

Use Optimal Seating Arrangements

Ensure good listening and active engagement during rug activities by making sure all students can see and hear what is going on. Use a seating arrangement that best suits the activity:

- **Form a cluster.** For a cozy setting, sit on a chair and arrange students in several curved rows on the rug right in front of you. Students will be close enough to note details in illustrations or photos, actively respond to questions, and chime in with the reading of a book or poem.

- **Create a horseshoe.** For a demonstration activity, arrange students in a horseshoe pattern, and seat yourself at the open end of the horseshoe. Use the interior area of the rug to spread out materials such as math manipulatives, science models, or historic artifacts.

- **Sit in a circle.** When holding a morning share time or class meeting, it is optimal to form a circle and sit on the rug knee to knee with your students. This will create a sense of community and convey to students your interest in listening and sharing along with them.

Keep All Students Engaged in Any Discussion

Many teachers have discussions with their students while they are on the rug. Use the same strategies presented on page 131 to ensure all students have a chance to be involved.

Another strategy to aid discussions when students are on the rug is to use a "talking stick" that is held by the student whose turn it is to speak. After the student with the stick is finished talking, the stick is passed to the next person who wants to speak. The talking stick can be a magic wand, baton, or ruler. Other items, such as a soft ball or small stuffed toy, can be used instead of a stick.

MOVING TOWARD SELF-MANAGEMENT

One Step to the Rug

Once students have learned to transition to the rug in the three steps outlined in this lesson, relax the procedure by simply telling students to go to the rug. Emphasize that the same behavioral expectations are in place: walk, sit in their own space, keep hands and feet to themselves, and no talking.

Let Students Sit Where They Want

When students have learned to be attentive while sitting on the rug, relax the structure by allowing them to sit where they want rather than in assigned spots. Remind them that the same behavioral expectations are in place.

Chapter 19

Independent Work

INTRODUCTION

The ability to work independently is critical to academic success. Students need to learn to focus on their work without distracting or disturbing others. They must learn to ask for help only after attempting the work on their own.

> ### BEHAVIORS TO TEACH
>
> During independent work time, students will:
>
> - Do the assigned work.
> - Stay in their seats.
> - Use their Help Cards.
> - Select an activity from the to-do list if finished early.
> - Do this without talking.

PREVENTIVE MANAGEMENT STRATEGIES

Get All Students on Task Before Helping Individual Students

When you give the students directions to start their independent work assignment, it is not uncommon for students to immediately raise their hands with questions. Do not be distracted. You need to focus your attention on monitoring student behavior, narrating those who are following directions ("Todd, Sharon, and Michelle are getting right to work."), and if necessary, correcting those who are off task.

After all the students are engaged, you can then answer any questions, begin helping students who need assistance, or both.

Continue to Monitor Student Behavior—Do Not Get Too Involved in Helping Individual Students

It is easy to become so involved in helping one student who is having trouble that you forget about keeping an eye on the rest of the students. Students notice if you are distracted and not withit. Never spend more than 1 minute with a student without looking up, scanning the classroom, and narrating or correcting student behavior if necessary.

No Talking Means No Talking

Independent work by definition needs to be done independently by the students. That means there should be no reason for students to be helping or talking to one another.

All too often the students will work without talking at the beginning of the independent work assignment but begin talking within a few minutes. Do not "shh" or give ineffective reminders if students start talking.

If students start talking, immediately narrate the behaviors of the on-task students. If this is not effective, approach the students who are still talking and correct their behavior.

Watch for Pseudo-Compliance

Some students will pretend to be working—but really are taking every opportunity to talk with their neighbor. The key to determining student intent is to look at their knees and feet. If the student's lower body is pointed forward, he or she is probably working. If his or her lower body is pointed toward a neighbor, you can assume talking will commence at the first opportunity (Jones, 2000). You will obviously want to take this as a cue that you may need to intervene.

Give Quick Positive Boosts to Students

While the students work independently, it is a perfect time to go around the room and make positive comments to them regarding how they are performing in the classroom. Keep the comments brief and make sure to comment on students who need that extra bit of attention.

BEST PRACTICES FOR INSTRUCTIONAL STRATEGIES

Give Effective Assignments

The quality of your assignments has a great influence on the success of the independent activities. Off-task behavior often occurs when students do not understand how to do the work or when the assignments are too challenging or not challenging enough. Keep these guidelines in mind:

- **Appropriate level of difficulty.** Choose tasks and materials that are at each student's appropriate instructional level. If the work is too difficult, students will become frustrated and disruptive. If it is too easy, they will quickly become bored.

- **Conduct structured practice.** Before you send the students to work on their own, have them practice the new skill with your support. For example, when you have them work on problems as a class, be available to answer any questions they have.

- **Check for understanding.** Often no student responds when teachers ask if the students have any questions after structured practice. Yet when the students get to work, the teacher faces a sea of hands. It is important to carefully determine if the students understand how to do the assignment.

    Have students give you a thumbs-up if they understand and a thumbs-down if they do not.

    Have the students pair off to see if their partner understands how they should do the assignment.

- **Let the students know you will check their work.** Assess their assignments with specific feedback. Make it clear that you spent time reviewing their work. Avoid one-word comments or single grades with no comments. Help students see and understand exactly what they can do to improve their learning. This will help them work more diligently next time.

- **Chunk assignments.** Break longer assignments into manageable "chunks." Tell students, "When you finish five problems, raise your hand, and I will check your work before you continue."

Use Help Cards

Have students use Help Cards during independent work time. Give each student or have each student make a tent card that can be easily seen when placed on his or her desk. One side is blank, and the other side has the word "Help" printed on it in a bright color. When a student needs your assistance, the student simply positions the card with the word "Help" on his or her desk where you can easily see it.

Do Not Spend Too Much Time Helping Students

The goal of independent work is to teach students to work *independently*. Therefore, try not to spend too much time helping them individually—you have too many students for that. Try the praise, prompt, and leave method (Jones, 2000):

- **Praise.** Comment on any part of the assignment the students have done correctly.

- **Prompt.** When giving a prompt, you simply direct the student to the next thing they need to do. You may want to quickly check for understanding to make sure students understand.

- **Leave.** Avoid lingering with individual students. This teaches them they cannot do it on their own, and if you become too distracted, the other students will take it as license to stop working.

Tell Students What to Do if They Finish Early

Have a plan for what students will do if they complete work early. Options can include:

- **A more challenging assignment.** Assign a second, more challenging assignment for those who finish quickly.

- **Silent reading.** It is a good practice for students to have one or two books of their choice at their desks or in their backpacks at all times. Be sure the books students select are at an independent reading level.

- **"When you finish early" list.** Develop a to-do list of activities students can choose if they finish an assignment early. Post this list in a prominent place in the room, and allow students to choose from a number of activities, such as double-checking their work, reading silently, or working at the computer or at another center. Update the list periodically to keep it fresh and motivating.

MOVING TOWARD SELF-MANAGEMENT

When students have shown that they can work independently according to your directions, consider giving them more flexibility in completing assignments in their own way. Try these ideas:

- **Have students help each other.** Have students help each other when they have a question. Tell students that they need to ask another classmate before they ask you a question. Allow students to talk quietly while they work together.

- **Allow students to work where they want.** As they work, allow students to stand up, lie on the rug, or walk around the room as appropriate to use classroom resources.

- **Expand the to-to list.** Eventually, the to-do list could include the option to do any activities you feel are appropriate.

Chapter 20

Working With a Partner

INTRODUCTION

Teamwork is an important life skill and many classroom activities lend themselves to working in pairs. However, when working with a peer, some students may use the opportunity to socialize, act silly, or otherwise avoid doing the assigned work. Since there may be from 10–15 different pairs working at one time, you can end up running from one pair to another responding to problem behavior rather than offering constructive instructional help. Making sure students learn how to work in pairs is an important prerequisite for their academic success in partnership activities.

BEHAVIORS TO TEACH

In the two steps to working with a partner, students will need to be taught several behaviors:

1. Pairing Off

When moving into pairs, students will:

- Move quickly to sit next to and face their partner.
- Speak in a quiet voice.

2. Working With a Partner

When working with a partner, students will:

- Sit with their partner.
- Speak in a quiet voice.
- Work only on the assigned activity.

PREVENTIVE MANAGEMENT STRATEGIES

Use a Two-Step Process When Students First Work in Pairs

When you initially have students pair off, there is a high potential for students to become disruptive. The more structured the transition, the better the chance it will go quickly and smoothly. Thus, it is useful to break the process into two steps. First have the students pair off and then, when they are settled, give them directions for how to work with their partners.

Use Simple Methods for Pairing Off

When you first have the students pair off, use simple methods. Pairing students with those they sit next to or across from often works best.

Let Nothing Distract You From Monitoring Student Behavior

When students begin working in pairs, let nothing distract you from monitoring their behavior and narrating or correcting it. Do not take any questions or become involved in any other activity besides making sure the students learn how to successfully work with their partners.

Make Sure Students Only Talk About the Assignment

Some students will try to use a paired activity as an opportunity to socialize rather than do the assignment. Monitor student conversations to make sure all students are making productive use of their time.

Work the Room

Avoid the temptation to spend too much time helping students, doing paper work, or preparing materials for another activity. When students pick up on the fact that you are not withit, you know what can happen! While students are paired off, keep moving around the room to monitor and give feedback to the students.

Avoid Partnering With Students

When you have students pair off, you may end up with one student who does not have a partner. Some teachers are tempted to partner with this student. Avoid this, since you will not be able to monitor the rest of the class. Instead, have this student join another pair of students and form a triad.

Help All Students Get Partners

Sometimes a class will have one student with whom nobody wants to work. Choose an empathetic, well-behaved student to work with this individual and praise that pair as they work together.

Give a Heads-Up to Students Who Have Trouble Working With Classmates

If you have a student who exhibits antisocial behaviors that alienate potential partners, pull the student aside before the activity and encourage him or her to display pro-social conduct that will make working with a partner more enjoyable.

BEST PRACTICES FOR INSTRUCTIONAL STRATEGIES

Teach the Social Skills Needed to Work With a Partner

Many students have not learned the appropriate social skills to effectively work with a partner. Before you have the students work in pairs, you may want to teach the students some basic social skills they will need to be successful. The ideas offered below come from Canter and Peterson's (1995) *Teaching Students to Get Along: Reducing Conflict and Increasing Cooperation in K–6 Classrooms.*

- **Be a good listener.** Developing effective listening skills is critical if students are going to work and cooperate with each other. These skills include being able to listen attentively to understand another person's point of view, feelings, or needs.

- **Give compliments.** Students often use sarcasms and put-downs in interactions with their peers. Unfortunately, many students have not learned the skill of making positive and complimentary comments to other students. Giving a compliment makes both the listener and the receiver feel good and helps to create a positive bond between them.

- **Express disagreements.** Many students do not have the pro-social skills to express disagreement with a partner. Teach the class some phrases they can use to *respectfully* disagree with a partner, such as "I don't think that will work, I would rather try _____," "What if we do this?" or "Can we try it this way?"

- **Take turns and share.** A lot of students have learned to only take care of what they want. Working with a partner gives students the opportunity to learn how to take turns and share.

Pair Students to Support Academic Success

Pair students up in a manner that will maximize the learning experience.

- **Weaker and stronger learners.** When students are occasionally paired in "weak-strong sets," typically both students gain. The more knowledgeable student practices thoughtfulness with the finest learning device—teaching. The weaker student profits from one-on-one attention, repetition, and perhaps a non-teacher approach that works.

- **Learning styles.** Pairs with similar skill levels may have different learning styles. For example, in math some students may solve word problems by drawing pictures; others may just do the work in their heads. Some may solve complicated math problems by writing down the steps first; others may have developed a method to remember the steps. After reading a question, one student may encourage another to look up an unknown word in the dictionary. These pairings can deepen understanding for both learners.

MOVING TOWARD SELF-MANAGEMENT

When students have learned how to work in pairs, you can try methods that promote self-management.

Utilize Different Methods to Pair Off Students

Have students choose their partners. In addition, you can try putting all the students' names in a container and pulling out the pairs.

Let Students Work Where They Want

Depending on your situation, collaborative activities can be made even more motivating when students choose their own locations for paired work. Allowing them to find a corner in the room, to sit outside the classroom, or stretch out on the rug demonstrates that you are interested in academic results, not just compliance with specific rules. Of course, basic rules still apply: Wherever they choose to work, students must stay on task.

Chapter 21

Teacher Works With a Small Group While Other Students Work Independently

INTRODUCTION

Having students work independently while you work with a small group—such as a reading group—can be one of the most difficult classroom situations to manage. While you work with a small group, students who are supposed to be working independently may often stray off task. Students need to learn to stay focused on their work when you are working with a group of their classmates. For this to happen, students need to follow the directions for all transitions and behaviors involved in small-group and independent work activities.

BEHAVIORS TO TEACH

Students need to master four areas in order to work successfully in this situation.

1. Transitioning to a Small Group

When transitioning from their seats to the small group, students will:

- Stand up quietly and push in their chairs.
- Bring necessary materials (reading book, notebooks, pencils, and so forth).
- Walk directly to the small group and take a seat.
- Make this transition without talking.

(continued)

BEHAVIORS TO TEACH (continued)

2. Working Independently

When working independently at their seats, students will:

- Do the assigned work.
- Save questions until the group's transition (use the Help Card).
- Stay seated.
- Work without talking.

3. Participating in Small-Group Instruction

When participating in small-group instruction, students will:

- Follow directions.
- Raise their hands and wait to be called on before speaking.
- Stay seated.

4. Transitioning Back to Their Seats

When transitioning from the small group back to their seat, students will:

- Take their materials and go directly to their seats.
- Get right back to work.
- Make this transition without talking.

PREVENTIVE MANAGEMENT STRATEGIES

Be Sure Students Are Able to Work Independently First

Working with a small group while the rest of the students work independently is one of the most difficult—if not *the most difficult*—activities to manage. Therefore, before you attempt this activity, make sure the students have demonstrated that they can work independently at their seats (see chapter 19 on page 138).

Have Students Begin the Assignment

Before you begin working with a group, take a moment to focus on students who are working independently. Make sure all students are settled and on task.

Sit Where You Can Easily See All Students

When you are working with a small group, you need to sit where you can scan the room and monitor the behavior of the students working at their seats.

Make Learning How to Work Independently Your First Priority for Students

At the beginning of the year when you have the students working at their seats while you are with a small group, your job is to make sure the students learn how to work independently at their seats. Make your top priority monitoring the students working independently rather than teaching the students in your small group. Until the students at their seats learn to stay engaged and quiet on their own, no meaningful learning will take place.

Continue Monitoring Students Who Are Working Independently

Students who are left to work independently while the teacher works with a small group are used to having the teacher ignore their behavior. They take it as a time to do what they want. Remember to monitor the behavior of independent workers. Every minute or so look up, scan the classroom, and narrate the behavior of students who are focused and silent: "Maggie and Caitlin are working on their own without talking."

Prepare Students for Any Transition

Give everyone a 2-minute warning before a transition. This will help students who struggle with organization or transition time to get ready to move.

Have Disruptive Students Sit Near You

Place students who may have difficulty working independently as close to you and the group as possible. Some students may need to sit apart from others to avoid being distracted or distracting other students.

Do Not Allow Inappropriate Talking

As in any independent assignment, there is no reason for students to be talking unless you permit them to quietly ask another student a relevant question. Avoid getting into the "shh" habit. If students are talking inappropriately, correct their behavior.

BEST PRACTICES FOR INSTRUCTIONAL STRATEGIES

Plan the Timing for the Activity

Avoid getting caught short on time. Plan ahead and develop a schedule for working with groups. First determine how long the instructional period will be, and then decide how long you will work with each group. Allow 2 minutes for students to transition from their seats to the small group and back. Here is an example of a 75-minute block for meeting with three different reading groups during a reading and language arts activity.

Group 1	9:00–9:23
Transition	9:23–9:25
Group 2	9:25–9:48
Transition	9:48–9:50
Group 3	9:50–10:13
Transition	10:13–10:15

Make Sure Students Can Do the Assignment

Make sure the task the students are working on independently is one that all the students can do without your assistance. If the task is too hard, students may become frustrated, be tempted to approach you for help, or become disruptive.

Determine How Students Can Get Help

Because other students cannot ask you for help when you are with a group, talk with the class beforehand about what they can do other than wait for you. With some prompting, students will come up with actions such as asking a friend for help (if you permit it), leaving the part they do not understand unfinished and moving on to another section, or trying the problem the way they think would be correct. Asking an aide for assistance would be another alternative, if you have one in your classroom.

Use Best Practices for Independent Work

Because the students at their seats will be doing independent work, the best practices suggestions from chapter 19 will also be useful for this activity (see page 138).

Chapter 22

Working in Groups

INTRODUCTION

The social and cognitive benefits of group work are well researched and extremely valuable (Johnson, Maruyama, Johnson, Nelson, & Skon, 1981). For many teachers, though, having students work in groups presents serious issues: They waste too much instructional time getting into groups, they socialize instead of work, they argue and cannot get along, or they simply do not participate. As a result, many teachers make the following conclusion: *Stay away from group work—the class cannot handle it.* The best group lesson plan will not succeed until students have learned to work effectively and behave appropriately in a group.

> ### BEHAVIORS TO TEACH
> When working in groups, students will:
> - Work on the assignment.
> - Stay seated.
> - Talk only about the assignment and in quiet voices.

PREVENTIVE MANAGEMENT STRATEGIES

Make Sure Students Are Ready to Work in Groups

A major mistake many teachers make is asking students to do group assignments before they have demonstrated they know how to behave successfully in activities that are less directed. Do not attempt to have students work in groups unless they have demonstrated an ability to get and stay on task during independent work and partner activities.

Keep Initial Group Experiences Short

When students are first put into groups, make sure the activity they engage in can be finished in a few minutes. The shorter the group experience, the more likely students will stay on task and not become distracted. As students demonstrate they can handle a quick group experience, you can begin providing them assignments that will take longer to complete.

Let Students Know You Are Monitoring Their Behavior

Remember not to spend too much time working with one group without checking on the behavior of the other groups. Let the students know you are monitoring their behavior. Every few minutes use a voice loud enough for all the students to hear to narrate the behavior of students who are engaged in learning, saying, for example, "The students in groups three and five are all working on the assignment using quiet voices." If students stay off task or are disruptive, approach them and quietly take corrective actions.

Continue to Circulate Around the Room

As you circulate around the room, keep your back to the wall and your eyes and ears on your students. Your presence alone will keep some students on task. If a few students have trouble working with their peers, be sure to spend as much time as possible in close proximity to them.

Have a Signal for Help

Be sure students know how to signal they need help. Review the information on asking for help in the chapter on independent work on page 138.

Establish a Signal If the Noise Level Becomes Too High

The noise level will rise when students work in groups. Establish a signal such as flashing the lights or ringing a bell that indicates the noise level is too high and students are to talk more quietly.

BEST PRACTICES FOR INSTRUCTIONAL STRATEGIES

Plan How You Will Place Students in Groups

How you place students in groups depends upon the purpose of the group. Place students who initially might have trouble working in groups with classmates who work well in groups.

- **Spontaneous groups.** Groups formed in the middle of a lesson may not require much planning. You could simply organize by table or proximity.

- **Ability grouping.** During academic activities such as reading or math, meeting student instructional needs must be the driving force.

- **Be flexible in the size of the groups.** At most grade levels, four or five students per group are reasonable. With low achievers, a smaller group may allow for more intensive instruction while a larger group of high achievers can still function well.

Review group makeup regularly with an eye toward forming new units to meet the current needs of your class. Avoid labeling your groups and keeping them together for months.

Carefully Explain Group Assignments

When the assignments are weak or do not have a clear goal, it is easy for students to find plenty of other things to do with their group. Explain the group's academic responsibility just as carefully as you explained the behaviors desired.

Have all students make different contributions to the final product. If the final product is a report, different groups could contribute the introduction, research, procedures, lab testing, and summary. Detail your criteria for success (a rubric, for example) and grade students on their individual contributions and group effort.

Use Engagement Strategies to Keep Groups Involved

Whether students quickly break up into informal teams or have ongoing group work as part of their day, the following engagement strategies will keep them participating actively. Adapt them as needed. In fact, you might involve your students in expanding these strategies. Here are two suggested strategies:

Hands-down idea sharing. Ask students to formulate some thoughts or opinions on a particular concept or idea. All of the group members can think (in silence, of course) about what they would like to say to their group about the topic. When each group member is ready to share, he or she places one hand down on the desk or table. When every member has a hand down, the group takes turns sharing ideas. This will get your quick thinkers and talkers to slow down and wait. It also encourages all students to contribute.

Media interviews. When students are working in groups, drop in and visit a group as if you were a TV or newspaper reporter. Respectfully eavesdrop and then politely stop the group's work to interview individuals about how they are doing in the group, what they have accomplished, and what roadblocks they face. Ask each student at least one interview question. Take a "commercial break" to interview one group that is modeling effective work habits in front of the entire class. Or, if a group is struggling, interview the entire class to gather suggestions from others.

Chapter 23

Working at Centers

INTRODUCTION

Learning centers provide an opportunity for students to work together or independently at a station dedicated to a specific activity. Centers also let you effectively use a limited amount of materials or equipment with all students in your class. For example, you may have only one microscope, but if you set up an experiment at a center, all students will be able to take turns during a hands-on investigation. Even the most compelling activities, however, can fail to result in learning if students use center time to play, talk, and stay off task. A great deal of responsible behavior is expected of students when they work at centers.

BEHAVIORS TO TEACH

1. Transitioning to a Center

When signaled to go to a center, students will:

- Stand up quietly and push in their chairs.
- Bring the correct materials.
- Walk directly to the assigned center and take a seat.
- Use a quiet voice.

2. Working at a Center

When working at a center, students will:

- Read the assignment first.
- Work on the assignment either by taking turns or as a group.
- Stay seated.
- Talk only about the assignment, and in a quiet voice.

(continued)

BEHAVIORS TO TEACH (continued)

3. Transitioning From One Center to Another

When signaled to transition from one center to another, students will:

- Take their materials with them.
- Walk directly to the next center and take a seat.
- Speak in a quiet voice.

PREVENTIVE MANAGEMENT STRATEGIES

Do Not Rush to Have Students Work at Centers

Some teachers feel that it is important to have students work at centers as soon as possible. Remember that the lack of structure presented by centers can be a serious problem unless students have demonstrated they can handle the independence.

Working in centers should be one of the last instructional activities that you have students engage in. Before you attempt this activity, make sure the students have learned to work independently in pairs and in groups.

Watch How You Group Students

Place students who initially might have trouble working in groups with classmates who work well in groups.

Let Students Know You Are Monitoring Their Behavior

For the first few times students are at centers, focus on helping students learn how to behave successfully. In a voice loud enough for everyone to hear, regularly narrate the behavior of students who are following directions and are engaged in the learning activity at the center.

Keep Circulating From Center to Center

This is an instructional activity that requires you to constantly move from center to center to ensure students understand directions and are staying on task. Keep an eye on students who have trouble with a lack of structure, and use your presence and attention as a preventive tool as necessary.

Cue Students Before They Are to Transition

Give students a 2-minute warning before asking them to move to another center. This will help them wrap up their work and focus on the upcoming transition.

Come up with a signal to indicate that students need to rotate to another center. Some teachers play a short musical piece. When the music stops, students must be at the next center and starting their work. A bell or hand signal can also be an effective cue.

Motivate Students to Quickly Make the Transitions

To prompt students to make the transition quickly, set a timer for 2 minutes and allow students to go from their seats to the centers. See if they can beat the clock without racing or becoming too loud. Remember to narrate the behavior of students who are on task during the transition.

Make a Path to Guide Student Movement From Center to Center

Help students find the next center by making a path on the floor leading from center to center. For example, you can use a line from the movie *The Wizard of Oz* by asking students to "follow the yellow brick road" to get to the next center.

Establish a System for Students to Ask for Help

Students are going to need help when they work at centers. Establish a system for students to indicate when they need assistance. One method you may find helpful is to provide each center with a colorful flag students can hold up to indicate that they have a question. An aide, a student helper, or the teacher can assist these students.

Separate Quiet and Noisy Centers

When planning and designing the centers, try to keep low-key, quiet areas some distance from the more active sites.

BEST PRACTICES FOR INSTRUCTIONAL STRATEGIES

Introduce the Centers With a "Preview Day"

Have the students join you as you tour each center and introduce activities or explain assignments. A preview day gives you the opportunity to highlight exciting activities as well as answer questions that might arise later when students work independently.

Supply Each Center With an Answer Key

When students finish, they can self-correct their work using an answer key. Not only does it provide immediate feedback, it also reduces the amount of paperwork to be graded.

Appoint Student Helpers

You may want to have student helpers assist peers during center time. Many teachers give these helpers a button or badge for identification. Each week the monitor can pass this duty on to a classmate who demonstrated appropriate behavior during center time.

Establish a System for Students to Record Their Efforts at Each Center

Whenever appropriate, put up a chart at each center for student completion or achievement. After completing a center assignment, students can record their progress in a visual way on the chart.

Have Students Carry Their Work in a Folder

In order to help students keep track of their assignments, give each student a folder that can be carried from center to center. This folder will help students keep track of work they completed during the week. At the end of the week, students select their best work to submit for a grade or they can submit the entire folder.

Use Clear and Simple Directions at Each Center

When students are working at centers, most of your direction to them will be by written instruction. In addition to ensuring that the reading and ability levels of these instructions are appropriate, be sure to use clear language and lead the students through tasks one step at a time. Your directions must be simple and specific.

Establish a System for Assigning Students to Centers

Use an entertaining visual aid to assign students fairly to each center. One example is to make a bicycle wheel out of cardboard with each student's name written on the spokes. When assigning centers, spin the wheel to select a student. Allow that student to select the center he or she would like to attend. Continue to spin the wheel until all students are at a center.

Part 8

Managing Procedures for Academic Success

Chapter 24

Introduction to Procedures

INTRODUCTION

Classroom procedures are basic routines that involve movement into, out of, or within the classroom. Transitions are often the hardest management issues most teachers face. The lack of structure that transitions present typically results in twice as much disruptive behavior by students as do other activities (Arlin, 1979). Due to the large number of transitions during a day or period and the time they often take to complete, some teachers lose up to 1 hour of instructional time per day struggling through transitions (Witt et al., 1999). When students know exactly how you expect them to behave during different classroom procedures, your school day will proceed more smoothly and you will have more time to *engage* in learning activities.

PROCEDURES

GUIDELINES FOR SUCCESSFUL PROCEDURES

Because procedures involve movement and movement involves time, you need to consider special factors when teaching students how to act during procedures.

Pay Attention to Time Spent on Transitions

To maximize the time for academic learning, minimize the time spent on transitions (moving from one location to another or moving between activities). Set a limit for how long a procedure should take: "I would like to see everyone lined up and ready to leave in 2 minutes." As the students learn your procedures, make it a goal to reduce the time it takes to complete them.

Give Directions Only When You Have the Attention of All Students

Because many classroom procedures involve student movement, it is important that all students hear your complete directions for what they are to do—before they start doing it.

Too often teachers begin giving directions when students are not fully attentive. The result is obvious: Some students—those who heard your directions—know what to do and start doing it; those who did not hear your directions do not know what to do and either do something else or start asking what to do. Either way, a smooth transition is lost and the teacher usually has to repeat the directions again and again.

Before you give directions, be sure you have the full attention of all students. This means they have their eyes on you and are not talking. Use your attention-getting signal (see chapter 25 on page 161) to get everyone focused.

Cue Students to Start

It is common for students to start moving before the teacher has finished explaining. The result is a frustrated teacher who exhorts students, "Wait a minute! I'm not finished with the directions!" Always tell students that they are not to start an activity until you have clearly cued them to begin:

> *"I do not want anyone to start until I have finished with my directions. Please stay where you are and do not start the activity until I say GO."*

Monitor and Give Feedback

When students are moving in or out of the classroom or from one activity to another, teachers often become distracted talking to students or preparing materials. It is critical that when students learn your procedures, you give your full attention to monitoring their behavior and giving consistent feedback through behavioral narration and corrective actions. Taking the time to monitor will make a big difference in how well students handle transitions.

Chapter 25

Attention-Getting Signal

INTRODUCTION

Throughout the school day, you will give students directions that they must hear, understand, and follow. Thus, you need to be able to get their attention quickly and consistently. An attention-getting signal cues students to stop what they are doing and give you their undivided attention. Effective use of an attention-getting signal keeps you from having to repeat your directions or make endless pleas of "Listen to me."

BEHAVIORS TO TEACH

When given a signal, students will:

- Freeze.
- Look at the teacher.
- Listen to what the teacher is saying.

PREVENTIVE MANAGEMENT STRATEGIES

Teach Students Your Attention-Getting Signal the First Day of School

Your attention-getting signal should be one of the first lessons you teach on the first day of school. Teaching students to be attentive when you speak is critical to the success of everything else you will do.

Use a Signal That Will Get Everyone's Attention

Make sure the signal is one that will get every student's attention. Signals could include:

- Flashing the lights.
- Ringing a bell.

- Giving hand signals, such as one hand in the air and the other hand with one finger on the lips (the "shh" sign).

- Clapping rhythmically: "When you hear me clapping, join in with me. When I stop clapping, you stop clapping and look at me and listen."

Expect 100% Compliance

All of your students must freeze and give you their attention when you use your signal. Remember to narrate behavior after you use the attention-getting signal, particularly in the first few days: "Chandra has her eyes on me and is not talking." Do not hesitate to correct any students who are off task or disruptive.

Use Eye Contact to Get Student Attention

When you give the signal, be sure to look directly at students who have difficulty complying. Your focus may be all it takes to get their attention.

Chapter 26

In-Seat Transitions

INTRODUCTION

Throughout the school day, you will often need your students to switch from one activity to another while in their seats. These transitions are not an opportunity to socialize, wander around the room, or become disruptive. Students must learn to move quickly and quietly from one task to another. Successful transitions are fundamental to a well-managed classroom that focuses on learning.

BEHAVIORS TO TEACH

1. Completing an Activity

When asked to clear their desks for a new activity, students will:

- Put away materials.
- Stay seated.
- Do this without talking.

2. Getting Ready for the Next Activity

When given directions to begin a new activity, students will:

- Take out materials.
- Stay seated.
- Do this without talking.

PREVENTIVE MANAGEMENT STRATEGIES

Use Attention-Getting Signal

Before you give directions for any transition, you must have the full attention of all students. Using your attention-getting signal (see page 161) will help you make sure all students are focused on you and listening to you.

Chunk and Model In-Seat Transitions for Younger Students

Present in-seat transitions in two steps. For younger students, model the first step and check for understanding before moving on to the next step.

Make Sure Students Have All of the Materials for the Next Activity

To make the transition between activities smoother and allow you to focus on the lesson, make sure students have all of the materials they will need for the next activity (see the chapter on distributing and collecting materials and papers on page 181).

Make Sure You Are Ready for the Next Activity

Keep the pace of the classroom moving. You do not want students sitting and waiting while you rummage through your briefcase or flip through files looking for the materials you will need to teach the next activity. Have all of the materials you will need for the next activity close at hand and ready to use to prevent down time that could lead to classroom disruptions.

Do Not Be Distracted by Student Questions or Comments

As soon as you tell the students to transition, some will inevitably raise their hands to ask a "vital" question. Be careful not to be distracted from monitoring the transition. Walk around the classroom as students put materials away and take other materials out. Continue to narrate behavior and use eye contact to motivate students who need a nudge. A smooth transition is as much your responsibility as it is the students' responsibility.

Have a Plan for Students Who Forget Materials

Some students will forget to bring materials back to school or will misplace them. Have a backup plan in place to handle this so time is not wasted and all students can stay on task. When students cannot find or do not have the right materials, let them borrow from an extra supplies cubby or share with a neighbor.

Assign Helpers to Pass Out Materials

Assign student helpers to be responsible for distributing supplies to certain areas of the classroom. If students are seated at tables, set up a stock of supplies at the table and have helpers distribute the supplies.

Give a Heads-Up That the Activity Is About to End

When students are immersed in learning, do not expect them to instantly stop and make a transition. Give a 2-minute warning—a cue that tells them that they will need to move to the next task in a short time. Prompt them to begin shutting down: "Now is a good time to complete the problem you're working on."

MOVING TOWARD SELF-MANAGEMENT

One-Step Transition

This chapter details how to teach the two steps of an in-seat transition. Eventually all directions may be given at once, and students may be able to use their own judgment regarding how to shift gears, such as whether it is appropriate to get up, throw away paper, talk quietly, or ask questions. For example, you may simply be able to say, "Let's put away our social studies work and get ready for math."

Chapter 27

Out-of-Seat Transitions

INTRODUCTION

In your classroom students will often need to get out of their seats and move from one work area to another. With 20–40 youngsters in a room, your clear directions will minimize the opportunities for your students to socialize, wander, and disturb others. Everyone needs to move quickly and quietly so that valuable learning time is not lost. Mastering this procedure is fundamental to your classroom's success.

BEHAVIORS TO TEACH

1. Completing One Activity

When asked to clear their desks for a new activity, students will:

- Follow directions to complete the activity.
- Stay seated.
- Do this without talking.

2. Getting Ready to Move

When given directions to prepare for a new activity, students will:

- Stand up and quietly push in their chairs.
- Wait for the signal to move.
- Do this without talking.

3. Moving to the Next Location

When told to go to the next location, students will:

- Follow directions.
- Walk directly to the next location.
- Do this without talking.

PREVENTIVE MANAGEMENT STRATEGIES

Do Not Allow Yourself to Be Distracted

Out-of-seat transitions are some of the most difficult management challenges. There is no way you will be able to move all of your students quickly and quietly from one location to another unless you give your total attention to monitoring the students, narrating their behavior, and taking corrective actions as needed.

Do not be distracted by student questions or by attempting to prepare materials. Loudly narrate the behavior of students who are following directions, and quickly correct any students who are not.

First Have Only Part of the Class Make the Transition

If the directions or movement patterns are especially complex, you may want only some students to make the transition at a time. You may start with half of the students making the transition first. When they have finished, ask the rest of the students to follow.

Loudly Narrate Student Behavior

Be sure to narrate the behavior of students who are following directions in a voice loud enough to be heard over the commotion of all the students moving around the room. By constantly using behavioral narration, you will be able to guide the students through the transition in a positive, quick, and quiet manner.

Closely Monitor Students Who Have Trouble During Transitions

You will soon know which students have trouble with the lack of structure in an out-of-seat transition. You must let these students know you are withit. You may want to have these students model how to follow the directions for the upcoming transition. This will move them closer to mastering the appropriate behavior.

In addition, you will want to keep an eye on the students as soon as the transition begins. You can either narrate their behavior or be prepared to immediately correct their behavior before it gets out of control.

Reward Students for Quick Transitions

Out-of-seat transitions can take up a good deal of valuable class time—the quicker they are the better. Set a time limit for transitions, such as 2 minutes, and then time students to see if they can beat the clock. If they succeed, give the class a point toward a reward. Extend the challenge by encouraging students to set a new and improved time record for quicker and quieter movement.

MOVING TOWARD SELF-MANGEMENT

One-Step Out-of-Seat Transitions

The ultimate goal is to have students make the transition from one location to another in one simple step. This may take time and practice, so remember to build this goal into your procedures. In time, students will be able to use their own judgment regarding how to behave during transitions, such as whether it is appropriate to throw away trash or ask questions.

Chapter 28

Lining Up to Leave the Classroom

INTRODUCTION

Before any substantial number of students can move from the classroom to another location (such as 15, 20, or 35 students), you will want them to line up. Lining up can be a time-consuming, disruptive experience with students rushing to get to the front of the line, pushing or shoving each other, yelling at each other, and so on. Students need to learn how to line up quickly and in an orderly manner before you attempt to have them walk in line.

BEHAVIORS TO TEACH

1. Preparing to Line Up

When told to get ready to line up, students will:

- Follow directions to get ready to leave.
- Gather materials they will bring to the line (lunch, sports equipment, books, and so on).
- Do this without talking.

2. Lining Up

When told to line up, students will:

- Quietly push in their chairs and walk to the end of the line.
- Stand in a straight line without touching anyone.
- Wait to be dismissed from the classroom.
- Do this without talking.

PREVENTIVE MANAGEMENT STRATEGIES

Allocate Enough Time

If you do not plan an appropriate amount of time for the students to line up in an orderly fashion, it adds to the potential disruptiveness of the process. Allocate adequate time before lining up for finding and putting on weather-appropriate gear. Younger students will need extra time to button or zip jackets and find mittens, boots, and umbrellas.

Stand by the Door

Give the directions for lining up while standing by the door. By doing this, you will place yourself where you can use your physical proximity to ensure student success.

Do Not Have All Students Line Up at Once

Initially, do not have all of the students line up at once—this can be very hard to manage. Pick one table or row to line up at a time. After students demonstrate they know how to line up, increase the number of students who line up by calling two tables, then four tables, or even all the students at once.

Some teachers pick students to line up by determining those who demonstrate they are ready, such as those who are sitting quietly with clean workspaces.

Have Students Who Struggle With Transitions Model How to Line Up

Be proactive! If you know students tend to be disruptive during transitions, have them model lining up. This will probably get the students in line without a problem.

Stay Withit

Lining students up is potentially one of the most disruptive activities you will ask students to do. Under no circumstances should you allow yourself to be distracted for any reason. Monitor the entire transition and do not forget to narrate students as they follow the steps of lining up.

Do Not Allow Students to Rush to the Front of the Line

If any students rush to the line or push to be in front, have them go back to their seats and wait for your signal again.

Assign a Student Equipment Manager

If needed, appoint a student to be the classroom equipment manager. Duties might include carrying appropriate materials, equipment, and clothing to designated activities. This student can also keep track of the equipment and ensure it is returned to the appropriate places after each use. Only after materials have been taken care of and accounted for should students be allowed to line up. (See chapter 47 on student helpers, page 235.)

Beat the Clock

Set a time limit—such as 2 minutes—for lining up as a way to challenge the class. Time the students to see if they beat the clock without rushing, pushing, or talking. If they are successful, give the class a point toward a classwide reward. Extend the challenge by encouraging students to set a new record by beating their previous time.

Teach This Lesson With the Walking in Line Lesson

You may want to teach this lesson in conjunction with the chapter on walking in line (page 172). Teach both lessons right before the class leaves the room for another location, such as recess or lunch, so students can apply what they have learned right away.

MOVING TOWARD SELF-MANAGEMENT

The ultimate goal of this lesson is not to teach students how to stand in a straight line—the goal is to help children learn to move quickly, quietly, and safely with their peers. Once your students have learned the basic structure to lining up you can help them move toward a higher degree of self-management. Here are some ideas:

- Have the entire class line up at once.

- Permit the students to talk quietly while lining up.

- Ask the students to try to leave the classroom in an orderly fashion without lining up.

Chapter 29

Walking in Line

INTRODUCTION

Moving a group of 20–40 children from one location to another on campus can be difficult. Without a procedure and clear directions, students may wander off, push or shove, or disturb other classes. Students can learn to move quickly, quietly, and safely in line as they make the transition across the school campus.

BEHAVIORS TO TEACH

When given the "GO" signal, students will:

- Walk directly behind the person in front of them.
- Keep their hands to themselves.
- Do this without talking.

PREVENTIVE MANAGEMENT STRATEGIES

Teach Students How to Line Up First

If students do not know how to line up in a quiet, orderly manner, it can lead to even more problems when you attempt to have them walk in line. Make sure the students know how to stand in line before you teach them how you want them to walk in line as a group.

Teach Students How to Walk in Line the First Time They Move as a Class

It is important that you teach the students how you expect them to walk in line immediately before the first time they are expected to use this behavior. Allow extra time so you can make sure you have time to have the students practice walking appropriately.

Assign a Line Leader and Caboose

Assign a student to be the leader. Make it clear that no one should walk in front of the leader. As well, assign a student to be a caboose at the end of the line and make it clear that no one should walk behind that student. The "caboose" student can turn off lights or shut doors after the class has exited.

Place Yourself Where You Can Easily Monitor Student Behavior

When the students are walking in line, position yourself so you can see all of them. Do not stand at the front of the line because you will have to turn around to check on the students. Most teachers find it works best to be at the back or to the side of the line.

Let Students Know You Are Monitoring How They Are Walking

When you first have students walk in line, narrate student behavior every minute or two in a voice loud enough for all the students to hear, such as, "Kyle and Dean are walking single file and are keeping their hands to themselves." When needed, correct students who are disruptive.

Keep Track of Students Who Choose to Receive Consequences

Many times teachers forget to bring a means to record the names of students who are disruptive and often forget to provide these students with the appropriate consequences. Students then quickly learn that nothing happens if you are disruptive out of the classroom. Avoid this situation by bringing a clipboard or other means to record the name of any student who chooses to be disruptive.

Have Students Who Need Support Walk Beside You

If some students are not following directions and are having trouble, you may ask them to get out of line and walk next to you.

Stop the Class if Students Become Disruptive

If more than a few students are not following directions, stop the class, go back to where you began walking, and have the students start again.

Chunk the Walk

When teaching students to walk in line, it is best to break the route into manageable chunks. Rather than walking all the way to the cafeteria, for example, have students stop and wait at a specified location: "Walk to the end of this hallway and stop." You can then provide behavioral narration, add any new directions, and keep things under control.

Buddy Up

Try pairing students up so they walk with a buddy. The line is much shorter when students walk by twos. This will also help eliminate stragglers and create a much more manageable line.

Teach Students to Keep One Foot on the Ground

Teach students to keep one foot on the ground at all times. If they concentrate on this, they will not be able to run!

Stop Before Entering a Building

Have students stop at the door before they enter the cafeteria, auditorium, return to the classroom, and so on. Once the class is stopped, you can then give directions for how you want them to behave when they enter the locale. (See chapter 30, Entering the Classroom After Recess or Lunch, on page 175 and chapter 33, Attending an Assembly, on page 184.)

MOVING TOWARD SELF-MANAGEMENT

When students have mastered walking in a line, you may want to have small groups of students—and eventually your entire class—go places without being in line if they can behave appropriately (no talking, bumping, or touching).

Chapter 30

Entering the Classroom After Recess or Lunch

INTRODUCTION

How you have students enter the room after recess or lunch communicates your expectations about learning and how time is spent in your classroom. If they are allowed to wander in noisily, take their time getting to their seats, and have nothing to do as they settle down, the message is that little else is going to happen—and that learning time is not particularly valued. Students need to move quickly and quietly into the room and immediately get ready to work.

> ### BEHAVIORS TO TEACH
> When returning to class after recess or lunch, students will:
> - Put away belongings and walk to their seats.
> - Start the assignment on the board.
> - Use their Help Card if they need help.
> - Do this without talking.

PREVENTIVE MANAGEMENT STRATEGIES

Determine When to Teach Students How to Enter the Classroom

Teach the students how you want them to enter the classroom at one of two opportune times: before leaving for recess or before leaving for lunch. This way the students will know the re-entry plan and can follow it when they return to the classroom.

Have an Assignment on the Board

Have an assignment on the board for the students to work on as soon as they enter the classroom. This will help students calm down and focus on learning.

Assignments on the board can draw or dispel student interest. A compelling task or interesting problem will increase curiosity and prepare students to learn. Some teachers designate an area on the chalkboard or bulletin board labeled "Problem of the Day," "Point to Ponder," "Do You Know?" or "Today's Journal Entry." Motivating, short solo tasks are your best bet. Silent reading for 5–10 minutes is also a good transition activity.

Expect the Students to Settle Down

Do not believe the myth that students must be wild after recess or lunch and cannot settle down. They can settle down if you expect them to. If students enter noisily, correct their behaviors—send them back outside, and have them come in again without talking. Immediately correct the behavior of any student who does not get to work right away.

Play Quiet Music When Students Enter

Some teachers find that playing quiet music when the students enter can set a tone that will help the students unwind and focus on learning.

Do Not Be Distracted From Monitoring Behavior

Lead the students into the room and stand at the front so you can monitor them. This enables students to observe your presence and hear your feedback. For example: "Jared has put away his jacket and has taken his seat. Miguel has started on his assignment."

When you are teaching students how to enter the classroom, avoid engaging in conversation with students that can distract you from monitoring behavior. Remind students that after they settle down to work, they can always use their Help Card if they need to speak with you.

Deal With Problems That Develop During Recess or Lunch at a Later Time

If problems arise during recess or lunch, students often will bring these back into the classroom and clamor to tell you what happened: "Teacher, he hit me!" or "Teacher, she called me a bad name." Do not reinforce this by dealing with it at this time. Have students use their Help Card if they have a problem, and tell them you will come around while they are working to talk with them. Here are suggestions for handling some common situations:

- There are reasonable ways to handle tattling. Unless a student is obviously hurt, tell him or her to write down what the other student did and hand the note in to you. You can also tell the students that they will have to wait until the next recess, lunch, or after school to tell you what happened. Most students will quickly forget the unimportant issues that arose with their peers.

- There is a difference between tattling on someone and *informing* an adult about someone. The purpose of tattling to a teacher is to put down classmates so someone will get in trouble. The purpose of informing an adult is to protect classmates so no one will get in trouble or be hurt. Illustrate this by bringing up a few sample issues and having students determine when it would be wise or unwise to tattle or inform. Give your students ideas on how to solve problems without immediately running to the recess supervisor or saving it for you.

- Another way to handle problems that come up during lunch or recess is to post a box inside the classroom door. Encourage students to write notes to you about issues or concerns raised while they were out of the class. Have them place these letters in the box as they come into the room. By establishing this system of communication early on, students will not stampede into the room eager to tell on a classmate.

Beat the Clock

Because entering the classroom after lunch or recess can take up a lot of time, it is best to set a timed goal—for example, 2 minutes—for the students to achieve. You can give the class points toward a class reward if they beat the clock. As the students become more proficient, you can lower the amount of time you give them to earn a point.

Chapter 31

Students Going to Pull-Out Programs

INTRODUCTION

Students will often need to leave your classroom for instruction at another location. They must learn how to leave the room quickly and quietly and head directly to the new area. When returning to the room, students must learn how to transition in an orderly, nondisruptive fashion, and get right back to work.

BEHAVIORS TO TEACH

1. Leaving the Classroom

When leaving the classroom to go to another location, students will:

- Walk out of the classroom.
- Go directly to their assigned location
- Do this without talking.

2. Returning to the Classroom

When returning to the classroom from another location, students will:

- Walk into the classroom.
- Take their seats and get back to work.
- Do this without talking.

PREVENTIVE MANAGEMENT STRATEGIES

Make Sure Students Know What to Do Before They Go to Pull-Out Programs

Teach students what to do before they participate in pull-out programs. This way they will be prepared and will know how to behave when leaving for and returning from the programs.

Make Sure Students Know When They Will Leave the Classroom

For younger students, put the schedule on the desks for those designated to leave the classroom. Show a picture of a clock with the time the students are to leave, and write down the days they are to leave the classroom. For older students, put schedules on the board or give a copy of the schedule to the students to keep in their desks or notebooks depending on the nature of the pull-out.

Schedule Pull-Out Programs to Minimize Academic Impact

If possible, try to arrange for pull-out activities to take place during the class time that students can most afford to miss. For example, while it may seem logical for a student to go to the reading specialist during reading time, he or she is actually missing out on the classroom instruction needed most.

Know Where Your Students Are

For safety and instructional reasons, it is important for teachers to know exactly where students are throughout the school day. To keep track of your students, provide tent cards (a piece of folded tag board) labeled with specific destinations. When the student leaves, the appropriate tent card is placed on his or her desk. With just a glance, you can quickly tell other teachers, paraprofessionals, parents, or other students the location of specific students. This is especially important during fire drills or calls from the office asking for a student. Older students might use a form on a clipboard by the door to write their name, their destination, the date, and the time of the pull-out program.

Acknowledge Students When They Return

When students return from a pull-out program, acknowledge them in a subtle but friendly manner. Welcome them back, thank them for coming in quietly, and let them know you are happy to see them.

Have a Buddy Help the Student Catch Up

Arrange for each student to have a buddy who will quietly explain anything important the student has missed. This buddy can also be responsible for taking extra copies of handouts to give to the student and for retrieving the student from the pull-out program, if needed.

Stay in Touch With Specialists

Communicate with the specialists who work with your students. Ask them for ways that you can help the students in your own classroom, and offer any information you have about your students that might be important for them to know. Think of yourself as part of a team in which each player is important to the student's success.

Chapter 32

Distributing and Collecting Materials and Papers

INTRODUCTION

A classroom day is filled with papers going back and forth. Disorganized distribution or collection of papers not only wastes learning time but could also result in your losing or misplacing papers. A clearly defined routine can help you avoid these unnecessary problems.

BEHAVIORS TO TEACH

1. Passing Out Materials and Papers

When materials are passed out, students will:

- Take just enough for themselves.
- Pass the rest to the next person.
- Speak in a quiet voice.

2. Collecting Papers

When papers are collected, students will:

- Place their paper on top of the other papers.
- Make sure the paper faces the same direction as the others.
- Speak in a quiet voice.

PREVENTIVE MANAGEMENT STRATEGIES

Plan Ahead

Have sets of work already in piles that roughly match the number of students in the row or table size. Pre-counting and placing the sets into groups of five or eight will help you quickly hand stacks to a person in each group.

Put clear labels or titles on top of the stacks of paper so you can refer to what is being handed out. If materials have titles, you can say, "Who still needs a copy of 'Making Words Plural'?"

Be Prepared to Help Younger Students

With younger students, you will want to walk around the desks or tables to keep a helpful eye on students as they place papers on top of one another. If younger students have trouble facing papers in the same direction, quietly give them a tip, such as, "All the name lines should be at the top."

Tips for Passing Out Materials

- Instruct students to turn around when passing papers to the person behind them. This can prevent a student unknowingly shoving papers into another's face.

- If students inadvertently take more papers than they need, have them carefully hold up the extras. That way, if a student still needs a paper after the stacks have been passed out, he or she can walk quietly to the student who is holding up the extra paper and get what he or she needs. Thus, the students are handling the resources themselves. If you collect and distribute the extras, you will add two more steps to the process.

- Have a designated space for extra materials. For example, when you are passing out a weekly homework assignment or newsletter, the extra handouts can be quickly and smoothly returned to the "extras" pile. When a row or group has been served, one student places the extras into the pile. You can sort this out at the end of the day when you need extra papers for absent students.

Constantly Narrate Behavior

Keep narrating student behavior as they distribute and collect papers: "William is putting his paper right on top of the other papers and facing it in the same direction."

Provide Reminders

Provide many reminders for students when there is, for example, an important paper they need to return the next day. Write the task on the board along with other homework assignments, and remind them of this important obligation several times on the day before the paper is due. You may want to pin reminder notes to their clothes or backpacks.

Collect Assignments When Students First Arrive

To help prevent loss, collect important papers (parent-signed slips and assignments, for example) as soon as students arrive.

Have Student Helpers

Assign a student helper or helpers to help distribute and collect papers.

Chapter 33

Attending an Assembly

INTRODUCTION

An assembly is a time for learning, entertainment, or both. Students need to know how to behave in an assembly just as in any other school activity. Unless students are taught how to behave, they will be inattentive or disrespectful of speakers, players, or performers.

> ### BEHAVIORS TO TEACH
>
> When attending an assembly, students will:
>
> - Sit in their seats.
> - Clap or respond only when appropriate.
> - Do this without talking (unless the assembly includes participation).

PREVENTIVE MANAGEMENT STRATEGIES

Determine Where Students Should Sit

Find out ahead of time where your class is expected to sit during the assembly. Check out the location if you have not been there already. You do not want to be leading your students blindly as you look for your designated area.

Practice With Younger Students

With younger students, it is a good idea to actually take them to the assembly location and practice how to behave before you go to an actual assembly. This will help them practice the transition as well as give them a preview of what to expect regarding filing into rows and behaving appropriately during a performance.

Make Sure Students Know Exactly How to File Into Their Seats

You may say to them, for example, "Walk down the row until you reach the first available seat and then sit down. Sit in the order in which you are lined up." If students are carrying their own chairs, make sure they understand your expectations for where and how they are to place them.

Let Students Know You Are Monitoring Their Behavior

You may not be able to give verbal feedback during an assembly, but you can still stay on top of behavior by letting students know you are keeping an eye on them. Scan the class frequently. If anyone is off task, use a look to get them back on task.

Remind Students That Your Rules and Corrective Actions Are in Effect

Be sure to let the students know that your discipline plan will be used to help students choose to behave during an assembly. Take a clipboard along so you can jot down names of students who choose to misbehave and follow up with them when you return to class.

Have Noncompliant Students Sit by You

Keep the students who may have trouble during an assembly as close to you as possible so it is easier for you to help them act appropriately.

Give a Classwide Reward for Positive Behavior

Tell students that you will be looking for appropriate behavior during the assembly and that you will be recording points for a classwide reward. Bring a clipboard and record the names of students who follow your directions. When you return to class, recognize these students and let them know they have earned points for their classmates.

Chapter 34

Emergency Drills

INTRODUCTION

Ensuring the safety of students is one of your most important responsibilities. In any emergency situation—earthquake, fire drill, stranger or disruption on campus, or dismissal due to weather—you and your students must know exactly what to do and how to do it. It is critical that you teach students the routines for various drills and the importance of responding to each situation in a calm and quick manner. Whatever the emergency, student safety begins with their listening to and following directions.

> ## BEHAVIORS TO TEACH
>
> When given a signal, students will:
> - Freeze.
> - Look at the teacher.
> - Follow the teacher's directions.

PREVENTIVE MANAGEMENT STRATEGIES

Learn Your School's Emergency Procedures

Emergency procedures and signals vary enormously depending on the size, location, weather, and potential risk elements of your school. Although all schools have school-wide policies in place, you must be proactive in determining exactly what they are, understanding them completely, and making sure your students are well practiced in following them.

Be the Last One Out of Class During an Emergency Drill

Never let a student be the last one to leave the classroom during an emergency drill or an actual emergency. *You* must be the last one out. Make sure the room is empty and close the door behind you. If students have practiced the procedures, they will be able to make the transition to the pre-assigned location without you leading them. If you have a classroom aide, he or she can lead the students.

Have Emergency Contact Numbers Available

Hang a clipboard by the door with your class list and emergency contact numbers so it can easily be grabbed on the way out during a drill or actual emergency.

Make Sure Students Understand How Serious Appropriate Behavior Is During an Emergency Drill

Always stress to students the seriousness of any drill. Because of the importance of the situation, you may want to impose the highest-level corrective action for misbehavior during a drill.

Chapter 35

Beginning of the Day or Period Routine

INTRODUCTION

The beginning of the school day or class period sets a crucial tone that can affect the rest of the instructional day. Students need to be taught the specific practices that will set up their day for achievement: entering quickly, putting away belongings, turning in papers, and getting ready to work.

> **BEHAVIORS TO TEACH**
>
> At the beginning of each day or period, students will:
> - Put away belongings.
> - Get ready to work.
> - Begin working.

PREVENTIVE MANAGEMENT STRATEGIES

Greet Students at the Door

Greeting students as they enter the room may keep you from doing paperwork or additional planning for the day, but the benefits far outweigh any consequences. Just as you would welcome someone coming into your home, checking in with students builds a personal connection. This is your chance to say a personal hello, note a new haircut, ask about an ill sibling or parent, or inquire about how the math homework went.

Have an Assignment on the Board for Students

Having a task written on the board to keep students quiet, seated, and learning is a positive way to start the day. Appropriate assignments to begin the day could tap student curiosity about what is to come or take advantage of an opportunity to finish an assignment. Silent sustained reading is always a good option, particularly if you have to make some additional preparations.

Do Not Be Distracted From Monitoring Student Behavior

There is a lot going on when students first enter the classroom. Be careful not to be distracted from monitoring student behavior, and be sure to narrate appropriate behavior. Make an effort to comment on each of the procedures you taught: "Tommy has put away his jacket and lunch, taken his chair down, and started to work."

Quickly Take Attendance

Taking attendance helps you learn who is who. You can assign this job to a student helper or monitor. Some teachers have students flip over an attendance card and initial it as they enter. Of course, taking roll yourself for the first few weeks will help you learn names and connect with your students.

MOVING TOWARD SELF-MANAGEMENT

As students demonstrate responsible behavior when arriving at class, you may choose to let them complete the goals (putting away materials, getting ready to work, and getting to work) in their own way as long as the goals are reached and general behavioral rules are observed.

Planning

Your beginning of the day routine will depend on many issues: your personal preferences, the age and abilities of your students, and the internal procedures and practices of your school. This lesson and the next differ from other procedure lessons in this book because they require you to assess your own needs before you teach the lessons. You will find worksheets on pages 190–194 to help you plan and teach the procedures you want your students to complete each day when they arrive in your classroom.

The planning activities have been divided into three parts:

Planning Worksheet 1: Determine the procedures students will complete each day.

Planning Worksheet 2: Divide the procedures among the three tasks: putting away belongings, getting ready to work, and beginning to work.

Planning Worksheet 3: Determine the behaviors you want students to engage in for each procedure.

After you have completed the worksheets on pages 190–194, you will be ready to teach the procedures.

BEGINNING OF THE DAY ROUTINE

PLANNING WORKSHEET 1

DETERMINE THE PROCEDURES STUDENTS WILL COMPLETE EACH DAY

What do you want your students to do before the instructional day begins? Depending on your circumstances and the age and needs of your students, you may or may not want to include various procedures in your routine. Check off the procedures below that you want your students to complete when they enter the classroom at the start of each day. Write any additional procedures on the lines that follow.

❏ Put away outdoor clothing.

❏ Put away book bags or backpacks.

❏ Put away lunches.

❏ Turn in homework.

❏ Get learning materials ready.

❏ Take down chairs.

❏ Sharpen pencils.

❏ Do their assigned jobs (if a student helper).

❏ Start the assigned academic activity.

Additional procedures:

_____

_____

_____

_____

_____

_____

_____

_____

_____

_____

_____

_____

Classroom Management for Academic Success © 2006 by Solution Tree
www.solution-tree.com

BEGINNING OF THE DAY ROUTINE

PLANNING WORKSHEET 2

DIVIDE THE PROCEDURES INTO THREE CHUNKS

There are three logical, overall tasks you will want all students to complete at the beginning of each day or period:

1. Put away belongings.
2. Get ready to work.
3. Begin working.

To teach students how to complete these three tasks according to your expectations, take the procedures you selected on Planning Worksheet 1 and divide them among the three goals. For example:

Goal 1: Put Away Belongings

This may mean students will:

- Put away outdoor clothing.
- Put away book bags or backpacks.
- Put away lunches.

Goal 2: Get Ready to Work

This may mean students will:

- Turn in homework.
- Do their assigned jobs (if student helpers).
- Take chairs down and be seated.
- Get learning materials ready.
- Sharpen pencils.

Goal 3: Get to Work

This may mean students will:

- Start an assignment.
- Read silently.

Use the spaces that follow to organize the procedures you chose into the three categories.

1. Put Away Belongings

This means students will:

_____
_____
_____
_____
_____
_____
_____
_____

2. Get Ready to Work

This means students will:

_____
_____
_____
_____
_____
_____
_____
_____

3. Get to Work

This means students will:

_____
_____
_____
_____
_____
_____
_____
_____

Classroom Management for Academic Success © 2006 by Solution Tree
www.solution-tree.com

BEGINNING OF THE DAY ROUTINE

PLANNING WORKSHEET 3

DETERMINE WHAT YOU WANT STUDENTS TO DO FOR EACH PROCEDURE

Next, determine the behaviors you want to see and hear from your students while they are engaging in each procedure. These will be the behaviors you will teach during the instructional section of this lesson. For example:

Procedure: Put Away Outdoor Clothing

This may mean students will:

- Put things away without pushing and shoving.
- Hang up jackets.
- Speak in a quiet voice.

Procedure: Get Materials You Need to Do Your Work

This may mean students will:

- Put pencils, books, and journals on their desks.
- Stay seated.
- Do this without talking.

Procedure: Start the Assigned Activity

This may mean students will:

- Work on the assignment on the board.
- Stay seated.
- Do this without talking.

In the spaces that follow, list the procedures you want your students to engage in and the behaviors you want to see and hear.

Procedure _____

Behaviors _____

_____

Procedure _____

Behaviors _____

_____

_____

Procedure _____

Behaviors _____

_____

_____

Procedure _____

Behaviors _____

_____

_____

Procedure _____

Behaviors _____

_____

_____

Procedure _____

Behaviors _____

_____

_____

Procedure _____

Behaviors _____

_____

_____

Procedure _____

Behaviors _____

_____

_____

Procedure _____

Behaviors _____

_____

_____

Procedure _____

Behaviors _____

_____

_____

Chapter 36

End of the Day or Period Routine

INTRODUCTION

Students need to end the school day in a calm, structured manner with plenty of time to clean up and organize their materials. A frantic last-second rush to leave can be upsetting and often causes students to forget their homework, personal belongings, and other materials. Students need to be taught how to end the day in a calm, constructive manner.

> ### BEHAVIORS TO TEACH
>
> At the end of each day, students will complete the following tasks by completing specific procedures related to each task:
> - Gather belongings.
> - Get ready to leave.
> - Leave.

PREVENTIVE MANAGEMENT STRATEGIES

Allow Enough Time for an Orderly End of the Day Routine

Set a timer to remind you to start the end of the day or end of the period routine. It is easy to become so involved in your lessons that you forget to start the schedule on time. When this happens, the result will likely be chaotic!

Do Not Be Distracted From Monitoring Student Behavior

Even with all of the activity that occurs when students get ready to leave, do not allow anything to distract you from monitoring behavior. Move around the room as students prepare to leave and be sure to narrate behavior for each of the procedures you taught: "Ari has put all of his materials away. Karyn has thrown her trash into the trash can."

Planning

Your end of the day routine will depend on many issues: your personal preferences, the age and ability of your students, and the internal procedures and practices of your school. This lesson and the previous one differ from other procedure lessons in this book because they require you to assess your own needs before you teach the lessons. You will find worksheets on pages 198–202 to help you plan and teach the procedures you want your students to complete each day before they leave your classroom.

The planning activities have been divided into three parts.

Planning Worksheet 1: Determine the procedures students will complete each day.

Planning Worksheet 2: Divide the procedures among three tasks: gathering materials, getting ready to leave, and leaving.

Planning Worksheet 3: Determine the behaviors you want students to engage in for each procedure.

After you have completed the worksheets on pages 198–202 you will be ready to teach the procedures.

Have Students Help Each Other Get Ready

If some students are on task and ready with time to spare, allow them to pair up with a student who needs organizational support. This will establish a sense of community and cooperation in your class.

Help Students Get Organized

For students with transitional or organizational challenges, create an end of the day checklist that can be laminated and either attached to their desks or displayed prominently in the room. Encourage individual responsibility by giving these students the task of using a dry-erase marker to check off each item when completed.

Use a Visual-Aid Reminder to Help Students

Use a visual-aid reminder as a checklist for students during the end of the period or day routine. Include reminders for homework, backpacks, clothing, special notes or forms, orderly desks and chairs, and so forth.

Say Goodbye to Students

Make the effort to stand at the door at the end of the day and say goodbye to students as they depart. A handshake, a high five, or pats on the backpack are good ways to express warmth. Just as you would walk a friend to the door when he or she exits your home, the same behavior in your class enhances your personal connection with students. This is also a good time for last-minute reminders and helpful hints, such as, "Check each math problem two times tonight, okay?"

MOVING TOWARD SELF-MANAGEMENT

As students demonstrate responsible behavior when leaving class, you may be able to let them complete the goals (gathering materials, getting ready to leave, and leaving) in their own way as long as they reach the goals and observe general behavioral rules. Once you relax your rules, pay attention to what students are doing and why. It may make you feel good to know that some students want to hang around because they appreciate you as a teacher and are comfortable in the room. Keep in mind, however, that others may hang around to avoid issues, certain people, or viable fears of going home.

END OF THE DAY ROUTINE

PLANNING WORKSHEET 1

DETERMINE THE PROCEDURES STUDENTS WILL COMPLETE EACH DAY

What do you want your students to do before the day ends? Depending on your circumstances and the age and needs of your students, you may or may not want to include various procedures in your routine. Check off the procedures below that you want your students to complete before they leave the classroom at the end of each day. Write any additional procedures on the lines that follow.

- ❏ Gather outdoor clothing.
- ❏ Collect book bags or backpacks.
- ❏ Pack empty lunch boxes.
- ❏ Review homework assignments.
- ❏ Pack appropriate homework materials.
- ❏ Put away personal materials.
- ❏ Put away classroom materials.
- ❏ Put up chairs.
- ❏ Do their assigned jobs (if student helpers).
- ❏ Clean out trash from desks and cubbies.
- ❏ Pick up trash around the room.

Additional procedures:

_____

_____

_____

_____

_____

_____

_____

_____

_____

_____

_____

END OF THE DAY ROUTINE

PLANNING WORKSHEET 2

DIVIDE THE PROCEDURES INTO THREE CHUNKS

There are three logical, overall tasks you will want all students to complete at the end of each day or period:

1. Gather belongings.

2. Get ready to leave.

3. Leave.

To teach your students how to complete these three tasks according to your expectations, take the procedures you selected on Planning Worksheet 1 and divide them among the three goals. For example:

Goal 1: Gather Belongings

This may mean students will:

- Collect outdoor clothing.
- Pack up book bags or backpacks.
- Pick up empty lunch boxes.

Goal 2: Get Ready to Leave

This may mean students will:

- Review homework assignments.
- Put away personal materials.
- Put away classroom materials.
- Do their assigned jobs (if student helpers).
- Put up chairs.

Goal 3: Leave

This may mean students will:

- Leave quickly and quietly.
- Exit the campus according to school policies.

Use the spaces that follow to organize the procedures you chose into the three categories.

1. Gather Belongings

This means students will:

_____
_____
_____
_____
_____
_____
_____
_____

2. Get Ready to Leave

This means students will:

_____
_____
_____
_____
_____
_____
_____
_____
_____

3. Leave

This means students will:

_____
_____
_____
_____
_____
_____
_____
_____

Classroom Management for Academic Success © 2006 by Solution Tree
www.solution-tree.com

END OF THE DAY ROUTINE

PLANNING WORKSHEET 3

DETERMINE WHAT YOU WANT STUDENTS TO DO FOR EACH PROCEDURE

Next, determine the behaviors you want to see and hear from your students while they are engaging in each procedure. These will be the behaviors you will teach during the instructional section of this lesson. For example:

Procedure: Gather Outdoor Clothing

Behaviors you might want to see and hear:
- Return to your seat with your clothes.
- Put all clothes on at your desk.
- Closet helper will see what is left behind.
- Do this without pushing or shoving.
- Speak in a quiet voice.

Procedure: Put Away Personal and Classroom Materials

Behaviors you might want to see and hear:
- Return pencils, books, and materials to their appropriate location.
- Remove trash from desks and place in cans.
- Speak in a quiet voice.

Procedure: Leave

Behaviors you might want to see and hear:
- Remain in your seat when the bell rings.
- Wait until you are called to line up at the door.
- Do this without talking.

In the spaces that follow, list the procedures you want your students to engage in and the behaviors you want to see and hear.

Procedure _____

Behaviors _____

_____

_____

Procedure _____

Behaviors _____

_____

_____

Procedure _____
Behaviors _____
_____

Procedure _____
Behaviors _____
_____

Procedure _____
Behaviors _____
_____

Procedure _____
Behaviors _____
_____

Procedure _____
Behaviors _____
_____

Procedure _____
Behaviors _____
_____

Procedure _____
Behaviors _____
_____

Procedure _____
Behaviors _____
_____

Classroom Management for Academic Success © 2006 by Solution Tree
www.solution-tree.com

Part 9

Establishing Classroom Policies for Academic Success

Chapter 37

Introduction to Policies

INTRODUCTION

Policies are behavioral expectations that are in effect at all times during the day or period. Policies can vary widely from classroom to classroom. No single list of expectations is appropriate for all classrooms, but many of the situations that require policies are common to most.

POLICIES

GUIDELINES FOR ESTABLISHING EFFECTIVE POLICIES

Determine Appropriate Policies for Your Students and Classroom

The planning sections of the policies chapters are different from those found in the instructional settings chapters and procedures chapters. Since there are many ways to implement most policies, you will be given suggestions to consider based upon the input of effective teachers, but it is up to you to determine the policy that best fits your needs.

Incorporate School-Wide Policies

Some policies your students will need to learn and follow cannot be developed without first referring to school policies. Those have not been included in this book. Typically, these include policies for behavioral expectations at lunch and recess, and before and after school. Find out your school's policies for these and other situations, and teach them to your students by applying the lesson format shown throughout this book.

Post Policies in the Classroom

Many teachers find it helpful to post some of their policies in prominent locations in the classroom. Classroom rules and corrective actions should always be posted because they are in effect at all times and in all classroom situations. You may want to post the behaviors you expect for sharpening pencils by the pencil sharpener and post your policy for making up missed assignments near a classroom bin for make-up work. If you have student helpers, you will want a chart that lists the different jobs, the name of the student responsible for each job (this will change from day to day or week to week), and how each job is to be done.

Monitor and Give Feedback

At the beginning of the year, it is especially important that you monitor how well students are following classroom policies and that you provide the appropriate feedback. Without consistent monitoring and feedback, students will not understand that the policies in your classroom are as important to follow as your other expectations.

Assess Your Policies

At the end of the first 2 weeks of school, evaluate the effectiveness of your policies. Ask yourself the following questions:

- Have the students learned to follow the policies?

- Is the implementation of the policy too time-consuming for me?

- Does the policy help the classroom day flow more smoothly?

Chapter 38

Classroom Rules

INTRODUCTION

In addition to behavioral expectations for specific activities, you need to teach students your basic expectations for how they should behave in your classroom. These expectations are called *classroom rules*. These rules are in effect at all times and help ensure that your classroom is a safe environment where you can teach and students can learn.

PLANNING

Determine Your Classroom Rules

Before the school year begins, determine the rules you want for your classroom. Begin by asking yourself, "What general behaviors do I need at all times, each and every day, so that I can teach and my students can learn? How do I expect students to conduct themselves in my classroom?"

In answering these questions, most teachers come up with the following basic rules:

Typical Rules

Follow directions. This is perhaps the most important rule you will establish. You cannot teach and students will not learn if the many directions you give throughout each day are not followed. Following directions is fundamental to a well-managed classroom.

Keep hands, feet, and objects to yourself. For students to have a safe and orderly classroom, they need to know they are protected from being hit, being kicked, or having their property taken or destroyed.

No swearing, teasing, or bullying. All students have the right to be in a classroom where they will not be verbally or psychologically abused.

Most successful teachers use these rules in their classrooms. Other appropriate rules might include:

- No eating in the classroom.

- No running in the classroom.

- No leaving the classroom without permission.

- No yelling or screaming in the classroom.

In selecting your own classroom rules, keep these points in mind:

Rules need to be observable. Address behaviors that you can clearly see. Vaguely stated expectations may mean one thing to one student and an entirely different thing to another. As a result, they are open to interpretation, are difficult to enforce, and often cause problems by opening the door to arguments. For example:

Observable Rules
Keep hands and feet to yourself.
No cursing or teasing.

Vague Rules
Be respectful to others.
Be nice.

Rules need to apply throughout the entire day or period. Classroom rules need to be in effect all day or period, no matter what activity is taking place. Avoid rules that may sound sensible but in reality would not be in effect all day. For example: "Raise your hand and wait to be called on before you speak." There will be times when students are expected to speak out, such as when in cooperative learning groups. Therefore, this is not an appropriate rule.

Teach Rules to Students

Students need to be taught the rules for your classroom. Because rules are in effect all day, every day, this lesson should be taught on the first day of school. Two related chapters, Positive Feedback (page 210) and Corrective Actions (page 213), should also be taught the first day.

Post Rules in the Classroom

Make a chart listing your classroom rules and have the chart ready when you teach the students your rules. Post the chart in a visible location in the classroom to serve as a constant reminder of the importance of the rules.

PREVENTIVE MANAGEMENT STRATEGIES

Send Copy of Rules to Parents

Send a copy of your classroom rules home to parents along with the corrective and positive actions that you will take if the rules are not followed. Parental support is vital. The more parents know what your expectations are, the higher the chance they will support you.

Change Rules if Needed

Do not hesitate to change a rule if it is not working. There is no rule that you have to keep the same rules all year long.

Rules Will Only Be Effective if You Enforce Them

Rules are meaningless unless you are prepared to motivate students to follow them. Be consistent. By definition, rules are in effect all the time. When students choose to break a rule, they also choose to accept a corrective action.

Remind Students That Rules Are in Effect at All Times

Tell students rules are different from the behaviors you expect them to engage in during the various activities in the classroom. You may want to emphasize, for example, that no matter what students are doing—lining up, working at centers, or working in cooperative groups—they are never to break the rule of no swearing or teasing.

It is a good idea, particularly at the beginning of the year, to review your classroom rules frequently. Use behavioral narration throughout the day to reinforce students who are following the rules and to remind other students who may be straying.

When a new student enters your class, use the opportunity to review the classroom rules for all students. Introduce the new student and have several volunteers explain the class rules.

MOVING TOWARD SELF-MANAGEMENT

Some teachers find it helpful to involve students in choosing some of the rules. Ask students, "If you were in the perfect classroom, how would students behave?" Keep in mind that many times student rules are stricter than those determined by teachers. Therefore, you should have a clear idea of the rules you would like to establish before beginning such a discussion with your students.

Chapter 39

Positive Feedback

INTRODUCTION

Along with teaching your classroom rules, you will need to tell students how you will give positive feedback when they follow those rules. Positive feedback is critical to motivating students to choose appropriate behavior, and it creates a positive learning environment.

PLANNING

Determine How You Will Provide Positive Feedback

There are two types of positive feedback that you will use: individual and classwide.

Individual positive feedback. This is the most effective form of positive feedback you can give to individual students. It is easy to do and can be integrated into any ongoing activity during the day. See chapter 9, Using Behavioral Narration, page 57, for more details.

Positive notes home and positive phone calls to parents. The goal of a positive note or phone call is to share good news with parents about their child. Telling students that you will send positive messages to parents about their good behavior is a great motivator.

Behavior awards. Special awards for appropriate behavior are always an effective motivator. Students will be proud to receive them and to take them home to show to their parents.

Classwide positive feedback. A classwide positive feedback system is a program in which all of your students work together toward a positive reward given to the entire class. The goal is to motivate students to learn new behaviors at the beginning of the year or to work on improving problem behaviors. You can choose from among many classwide positive feedback systems. A simple system to use at the beginning of the year is called points-on-the-board (see chapter 9, Using Behavioral Narration, page 57, for details).

Tell Students How You Will Provide Positive Feedback

Right after teaching your rules, on the first day of school, tell the students how you will give them positive feedback if they follow the rules.

Post How You Will Provide Positive Feedback

Post how you will provide positive feedback in a prominent location in the classroom. Most teachers post this in the same location where they list their class rules.

PREVENTIVE MANAGEMENT STRATEGIES

Prepare Notes and Awards Ahead of Time

Plan ahead by copying a number of blank behavior awards and positive notes. Having awards or notes on hand makes it easier to consistently give them to deserving students.

Remember that handwritten notes—even short comments—that let students know you noticed their behavior are much more influential than a quick signature on a preprinted form.

Recognize Every Student Each Day

Set yourself a goal to recognize every student each day in a positive way. Some teachers keep a class list close at hand and place a check mark by student names each time they receive positive recognition.

Be fair and sincere. Students sense when praise is artificial or overdone. They also notice if you tend to reward certain students more than others. Think about the comments that help you feel valued and important, and make a sincere effort to treat your students in a similar manner. Narrating desirable behavior is always preferable to giving empty praise.

Make Positive Contact With the Parents of at Least Two Students Each Day

Positive contact with parents can yield positive results. Many teachers set a goal for themselves to contact two parents each day with positive news. When parents hear positive news instead of problem news about their child, you are much more likely to gain their ongoing support.

Motivate Noncompliant Students With Positive Peer Pressure

Catch noncompliant students when they are following directions and make sure they earn points toward the classwide reward (see chapter 9, Using Behavioral Narration, on page 57).

The more these students earn points, the more the other students will encourage them to behave. This type of positive peer pressure is a great motivator for older students.

Keep Your Positive Feedback Fresh

Keep your positive recognition fresh throughout the year. The same award handed out over and over will soon lose effectiveness. By being creative in the ways you recognize students, they will work harder to achieve the goals you set for them.

Change your classwide reward system from time to time. For example, instead of giving students points for following directions, put a marble in a jar when students behave. Tell the class that they will earn a reward when the marbles reach a certain level. Variety will help students remain motivated.

MOVING TOWARD SELF-MANAGEMENT

At the beginning of the year, it is important to use both individual and classwide positive feedback systems. As students learn to follow the rules, many teachers find they no longer need to use a classwide reward system to motivate students to behave appropriately.

Chapter 40

Corrective Actions

INTRODUCTION

No matter how effectively you teach students to meet your behavioral expectations, some will not meet them right away. You must have a clear policy for the corrective actions you will take when misbehavior occurs. Without a policy, you will be forced to constantly make choices about how to react. These on-the-spot responses are often arbitrary, inconsistent, and based on emotion. Planning out the corrective actions you will take before the school year begins will increase the consistency and effectiveness of your responses.

Students benefit as well from having a clear policy concerning how you will respond to their misbehavior. They have a right to know that they will be treated fairly when they misbehave. A set policy gives all the students a clear picture of the corrective actions they can expect you will take.

PLANNING

Determine Corrective Actions to Use When Students Choose Not to Follow the Rules

Here are some guidelines to follow:

Corrective actions should be designed to help students learn from their mistakes. The goal of corrective actions is not to punish students. You would never punish a student for a mistake in reading or math, so why would you punish a student when he or she misbehaves? Effective corrective actions are designed to help teach students appropriate behavior.

Corrective actions must be something that students do not like, but they must never be physically or psychologically harmful. A corrective action should never intentionally embarrass, humiliate, or physically harm any student. However, a corrective action will not be effective unless it is something the students find undesirable, such as losing recess time.

Corrective actions do not have to be severe to be effective. Teachers often think that the more severe the corrective action, the more impact it will have on a student. This is not true. The key to effective corrective action is that it must be used consistently. It is the inevitability of the corrective action and not the severity that makes it effective. Here are typical consequences teachers find effective:

Time out (removing a student from the group). Removing a student from the group is an effective corrective action for elementary age students. Designate a chair or table as the time-out area. Depending on the age of the student, a trip to the time-out area could last from 5–10 minutes. While separated from the rest of the class, the student continues to do his or her class work.

Staying 1 or 2 minutes after class. With older students, a good consequence is to simply have them wait 1 or 2 minutes after the other students have been dismissed for the next class period or recess, for example. One or 2 minutes may not seem like a lot of time, but it can be an eternity to students who want to walk to the next class with their friends or be the first in line for handball.

During the 1- or 2-minute wait, you can take the opportunity to briefly counsel the students regarding how you can work together to help them make better choices regarding their behavior.

Think sheet. The purpose of a think sheet is to encourage the student to think about misbehavior. You may want students to take the think sheet home for parents to sign and return. The student should write the following on the think sheet:

- The rule that was broken.

- Why the student chose to break the rule.

- What the student could do differently next time.

Time out in another classroom. This corrective action entails sending the student to *another* classroom for approximately 20 minutes with academic work to complete. This is a useful corrective action, especially if you do not have administrative support. Make arrangements with the teacher in that classroom beforehand, and place this corrective action at the appropriate level on your hierarchy.

Immediate call to parents. Calling parents with the student present at the next available break after a student misbehaves can be a powerful corrective action. Such immediate action can have a strong impact. If necessary, call the parents at work. If your classroom does not have a phone, use your own cell phone.

Corrective actions should be organized in a hierarchy. The best way to use corrective actions is to organize them into a hierarchy. A hierarchy lists the corrective measures in the order in which they will be imposed for inappropriate behavior during a day or period.

A hierarchy is progressive and starts with a reminder. Corrective actions in the hierarchy then become gradually more substantial for the second, third, fourth, and fifth times that a student chooses to misbehave. Here is how a 1-day hierarchy might work.

> The **first time** a student misbehaves, simply remind the student of the directions that were to be followed: *"Cary, the direction was to take out your social studies book and read pages 46 through 51 without talking."*

> The **second time** may warrant a few minutes of reflection time away from the group.

> The **third time** could lead to a conference with the student during recess, or the student could fill out a think sheet that helps him or her come up with alternatives to the misbehavior.

> If a student misbehaves **four times** in a day, consider contacting the parents.

> Finally, if a student misbehaves **five times**, send the student to the administrator's office.

When using a hierarchy, do not carry over the corrective actions into the next day. Students should start each day with a clean slate.

However, your hierarchy should include a severe clause to use when a student becomes defiant or violent. In such cases, skip all of the other steps and send the student directly to the administrator's office.

Sample Hierarchy	
First Disruption:	Verbal reminder
Second Disruption:	5 minutes away from the group
Third Disruption:	Fill out a think sheet or conference with the teacher
Fourth Disruption:	Call parent or send home a think sheet for parent to sign
Fifth Disruption:	Send to principal's office
Severe Clause:	Send to principal's office

Keep track of corrective actions. For your hierarchy to be simple to use and easy to integrate into your teaching routine, you will need a system to keep track of student misbehavior and the corrective actions accrued each day. You will need to know at a glance the names of students who have received corrective actions and where they are in the hierarchy. Keeping track does not have to be time-consuming, nor does it have to interrupt your teaching. Here are some suggestions:

Write names of students on a clipboard. The first time a student misbehaves, write his or her name on your clipboard. If the student misbehaves again, put a check next to his or her name and continue doing so each time the misbehavior occurs. At a glance you will know how far down on the hierarchy each student has gone and the corrective actions the student has chosen. Place a blank sheet on the clipboard each morning.

Use a color-coded card system. Make a chart of student names with a pocket under each name. Put five different colored cards in the pocket. Each color signifies a different place on the hierarchy. For example:

Sample Color-Coded Card System	
Green	No corrective actions
Blue	First time student misbehaves
Yellow	Second time student misbehaves
Orange	Third time student misbehaves
Red	Fourth time student misbehaves
Purple	Fifth time student misbehaves

At the beginning of the day, all students have green cards showing in the pocket under their name. The first time a student misbehaves, you or the student moves the green card to the back of the deck leaving the blue card showing. This indicates the student has received a reminder. Each successive time a student misbehaves, the front card goes to the back, exposing the card that indicates where the student is on the hierarchy. At the end of the school day, a student helper can put all the cards back in order for the beginning of the next day.

PREVENTIVE MANAGEMENT STRATEGIES

Teach Students What Your Corrective Actions Will Be the First Day

Teach this lesson on the first day of school along with the chapters on classroom rules (page 207) and positive feedback (page 210). The students will immediately want to know what will happen if your classroom rules are not followed.

Send Copies of Your Discipline Hierarchy to Parents

Parental support is vital to helping you create a classroom that promotes academic success. Parents need to know what steps you will take to help their children make positive choices in the classroom. Therefore, you need to send home a copy of your discipline hierarchy to parents. You may have the parents sign a form to indicate they have read the hierarchy and discussed with their child how they expect him or her to behave in your class.

Give a Copy of Your Discipline Hierarchy to Your Administrators

You will need administrator support with some of your noncompliant students. Teachers who are effective at getting support from administrators find that it is helpful to let the administrators know how they will try to handle student misbehavior before they need to send a student to the office. Discuss your plan with your administrators and determine what their course of action will be when students are sent to them.

Be Prepared for Students to Test You

Students *will* test you. After the first few days of school, some of them may begin to openly misbehave to see if you mean business about taking corrective action. If you do not consistently follow through and correct student behavior when appropriate, you might be in for a long year. Be firm and consistent.

Chapter 41

Bringing Appropriate Materials to Class

INTRODUCTION

Students need to learn that they are responsible for bringing the appropriate learning materials to class. When students do not have the needed materials, the time you spend finding temporary replacements will disrupt or slow down instruction. Students need to know what you expect them to bring to class and what will happen if they do not follow these instructions.

PLANNING

Determine Your Policy for Bringing Materials to Class

Let students know exactly what they need to have with them each day. You may also want to establish a policy for corrective actions when students forget materials.

Some teachers have corrective-action hierarchies that apply directly to bringing materials to class. Because students are likely to leave their books and materials at home at least once, these hierarchies typically begin with a warning. See the Sample Policy feature on the next page.

Note: Use your best judgment in working with students who forget materials. Some homes are so chaotic that it is difficult to hold students accountable—particularly young children—for bringing things back to school. Do your best to involve parents. If your efforts are unsuccessful and books are not returned, you may choose not to send materials home at all.

Other Corrective Actions

If a student needs to borrow materials, this wastes the time of the entire class. The student can pay back the time at recess (1 minute may be a reasonable amount of time for borrowing materials).

Some teachers count students tardy if the student has to leave the classroom to get materials left in a locker or on the playground.

Sample Policy

1st and 2nd grades

First time without materials	Warning
Second time without materials	Send a note home or call parent. The objective is not to be punitive, but to ask parents to help make sure needed materials are in the student's backpack.

3rd grade and above

First time without materials	Warning
Second time without materials	Sit out one recess.
Third time without materials	Call home again and ask parents to help make sure the student has needed materials when leaving for school in the morning.

Determine the length of time the hierarchy will cover—1 day or 1 week—before starting over.

Some teachers take no corrective action. They simply give students extra books or pencils. The goal is to get students working, and in some cases simply providing the supplies may be the best solution.

PREVENTIVE MANAGEMENT STRATEGIES

Send Classroom-Materials Policy Home to Parents

Send your policy home with students so parents will know your expectations. Parents need to understand that having materials in class is important to their child's progress. If applicable, let parents know the corrective actions you will take when students do not have the appropriate materials.

Young students often have a hard time remembering to bring materials back to school. This may be a losing battle if parents are not involved in helping them. Some teachers simply do not send books home with younger students because it is so difficult to get them back and often unfair to hold the students responsible.

Put Student Names in Their Books

Make sure the student's name is written in his or her books. This will help students keep track of their materials and discourage students from taking books that do not belong to them.

If you cannot write the names in the books, then try numbering all textbooks in permanent marker on the inside cover. Then write student names on a list with the corresponding number listed beside each student's name.

Have a Plan for Borrowing or Sharing Materials

Because it is inevitable that students will forget materials from time to time, have a plan in place for borrowing or sharing materials.

Let Students Know What Items Should Not Be Brought to Class

When you prepare students to bring appropriate materials to class, also make sure to specify any items that are *inappropriate,* such as toys and electronic devices. Ask students why these items might be disruptive to learning. If a student brings an inappropriate item to school, then have a designated safe place to keep the item until dismissal.

Give Students Tips to Help Remember the Materials They Need

Teach students to come up with tricks that will remind them to take the materials they need each day for class. Some ideas to share include putting a sticky note on the inside of their front door or on the mirror in their bathroom that reminds them to take their materials to class. Ask students to brainstorm other ideas and have them select one that will help them remember to take their materials to class.

Classwide Reward System

You may want to organize a classwide reward system for bringing materials to class. For example, if 100% of students remember to bring all of their materials, the class would earn a small reward. Be sensitive to those students, particularly younger ones, who may have little control over returning materials to school.

Establish a Behavior Contract With Some Students

Develop an individual motivation plan for students who regularly fail to bring materials to class. For example, let them earn a special privilege if they remember to bring their materials for 1 week.

Chapter 42

Making Up Missed Work Due to Absence

INTRODUCTION

Absent students are everyday facts of school life. You *and* your students need to know your expectations for making up missed work. Students will need to know what they are required to make up and how long they have to do it.

PLANNING

Determine Your Policy for Making Up Work Missed Due to Absence

Keep in mind that students may not be able to make up some work until they are caught up with the instruction that was missed. In your planning, you need to remember that you may have to work with a student individually before assignments can be made up.

Here are ideas to consider:

Make-up work folders

- Number a set of folders so that you have one numbered folder for each student in your class. By numbering the folders instead of writing names on them, you can reuse the folders each year. Assign each student a number and keep a corresponding list. For younger students you may need to write names on the folders.

- Depending on the age of your students, you may want to post a number and name list near the make-up work folders bin.

- Place the folders in an easily accessible bin.

- When a student is absent, place the work that needs to be made up in his or her folder.

- When the student returns to class, the student can pick up his or her folder and know exactly what work needs to be done.

Homework buddies

- Group students into pairs or teams called "homework buddies."

- When a student is absent, his or her buddy is responsible for writing down all missed assignments, bulletins, and homework.

- Make a form that students can use to write down all missed assignments, and make a folder for storing homework.

- Designate a location where students can place their partner's folder at the end of each day.

- If appropriate, have the students take the folder to their partner's house.

Internet

- You may be able to email students about missed work if you have a computer in your room with an email account and know that some students have email at home.

- If you do not have the time to do this, enlist a student to send the message (perhaps the absent student's homework buddy or a student helper). Of course, make sure students know to check for email. You obviously will not be able to use this system with all of your students.

- Many schools use a homework hotline or post all assignments on a web site that is accessible to students and parents from home. This way, students do not have to wait till they come back to school to get assignments.

Keep These Tips in Mind When Having Students Make Up Work

- Determine how long a student has to complete the work on a case-by-case basis. Consider the age of the student, how long the student was out, the nature of the work that was missed (new concepts or reinforcement), and the student's current workload.

- Not all homework may need to be made up. It can be hard enough to catch up without being overloaded. Give careful thought to the value of each assignment you ask a student to make up.

- If a student is absent for a significant length of time, a parent may pick up the folder or a friend can take it home to the student.

PREVENTIVE MANAGEMENT STRATEGIES

Send Policy to Parents

Send a note home to parents explaining your policy for making up work. Ask that they help their children catch up when returning to school after an absence. In some cases, you may want to have parents sign and return the make-up work.

Add Make-Up Work to Folders Each Day

Add make-up work to folders each day of an absence as you give out assignments—this way you will not have to scramble later to find the assignment.

Set Aside Time to Help Students

Do not frustrate students by expecting them to make up work they do not understand because they missed the lesson. When they return to school, pull them aside (during free reading or group time) and give them a mini-lesson. Depending on the age of the student and the nature of the work missed, you may want to do the homework together. If the homework is reinforcement, it can probably go home with the student. If it covers new concepts, you may want to work through it with the student.

If your school has an after-school tutoring program, encourage students to go to a tutoring session to review anything they may have missed during their absence. If possible, create a peer tutoring program that is available during recess, during lunch, or after school. If time allows, incorporate peer tutoring into group work throughout the day.

Chapter 43

Sharpening Pencils

INTRODUCTION

Without a clear policy for sharpening pencils, you may experience a number of problems: interrupted lessons, students unable to work because they do not have a usable pencil, a long line of students waiting to use the sharpener, and an all-too-compelling excuse for students to keep jumping out of their seats to sharpen and re-sharpen pencils. You need to develop a simple plan that covers how and when pencils will and will not be sharpened.

PLANNING

Determine Your Policy for Sharpening Pencils

There is no one-size-fits-all policy. Come up with a policy that works for you and your students. Here are two options:

Let students sharpen their own pencils. If you want to have students sharpen their own pencils and avoid noisy interruptions at the same time, you need to determine the following:

When can students use the pencil sharpener?

Some teachers set up specific times for pencil sharpening, such as when students first arrive in the classroom each morning or at the beginning of the period or day. Other teachers allow students to use the sharpener when they work independently. Sharpening pencils during classroom instruction should not be allowed.

How many students can use the sharpener at a time?

A long line of students invites disruption in the classroom. Two students at a time—one at the sharpener, the other waiting—is a good place to start.

Have a pencil monitor sharpen all pencils. Many teachers designate one student as the pencil monitor. There are a number of distinct advantages to this, not the least of which is that having a monitor alleviates the problem of students breaking pencil points intentionally so they can get up and go to the sharpener.

Use the "can" technique. Perhaps the simplest and most effective way of organizing the job of pencil monitor is the "can" technique. A can full of sharpened pencils is kept in a central location in the classroom. Another can sits nearby for dull pencils. Depending on your classroom situation, you may want to place similar sets of pencil cans at each table of students.

When a student needs a sharpened pencil, he or she places the dull one in the dull pencils container and takes a sharp one from the sharp pencils container. At the end of the day—or whenever you decide is best—the pencil monitor is responsible for sharpening the dull pencils and placing them in the sharp pencil container.

If you choose to use cans, consider dividing your class into smaller, more manageable groups (designated by table, corner, or a special name). Assign a pencil monitor for each group to be in charge of sharpening pencils.

PREVENTIVE MANAGEMENT STRATEGIES

Watch for Deliberate Pencil Breakers

Some students will deliberately break pencil points just to have an opportunity to get up and use the pencil sharpener. Keep this in mind if your policy allows students to sharpen their own pencils.

Pass Out and Collect Pencils

If having and keeping an adequate supply of pencils is a problem, pass them out and collect them each day.

Some teachers allow older students to bring mechanical pencils to class. This alleviates the need to sharpen pencils at all in some classrooms.

Be Sure Students Know How to Properly Sharpen Pencils

Do not assume that all students, even older ones, know how to sharpen a pencil properly. If appropriate, give a brief demonstration and offer helpful tips such as advising students not to make the points too sharp—doing so causes the lead to break easily.

Personalize Pencils

Personalizing pencils by placing stickers at the eraser end is especially effective for helping younger students keep track of and take care of their pencils.

Assess Effectiveness of Your Policy

If the pencil system you have established is working well, tell students how pleased you are with their cooperation. Be specific about the behaviors that are contributing to the success of the system.

If the pencil system you have established is not working, ask students what they think needs to be improved. Instead of instituting your own new policy, help students buy into the changes enthusiastically by giving them a role in creating a new policy that works for everyone.

Chapter 44

Using Materials on Bookshelves or in Cabinets

INTRODUCTION

Many of the materials students use during the day or period—books, scissors, paper, art supplies, and games—are kept for shared use in cabinets or on bookshelves. In order for these materials to be used and maintained properly and to prevent their use from impacting the flow of instruction, you need to establish a policy regarding when and how students can access the materials.

PLANNING

Determine Your Policy for Using Classroom Materials

Some teachers prefer to have each student get his or her own materials. Others prefer to have classroom monitors distribute and collect materials. Depending on the activities, you may want to use both strategies and choose the one best suited for each activity. The following guidelines will help you implement each strategy:

Students take and return their own materials. If you want to have students borrow and return materials on their own, you need to answer these questions:

When can students get materials?

Some teachers set up specific times such as the beginning of the period or the end of the day. Other teachers allow students to use materials only when necessary to work on an identified project. Students should never be allowed to disturb instruction with trips to and away from storage areas.

How are materials returned?

Students need to return materials at a time when they will not disrupt the class. Materials should also be put back the way they were found.

Student helpers distribute and collect materials. Many teachers assign students the job of distributing and collecting materials. If students need books from the shelves, three or four monitors gather the books and pass them out. If an art project requires scissors, the helpers place a can of scissors at each table area.

PREVENTIVE MANAGEMENT STRATEGIES

Label and Organize

The better organized your classroom is, the easier it will be for students to use and return materials appropriately:

- Label storage bins with words (or with pictures for younger students).

- Place frequently used books on convenient, easy-to-reach shelves.

- Put papers into bins rather than stacking them on shelves.

- Store scissors, markers, and so forth inside cabinets.

- Have a check-out system for your classroom library (see below).

Color Code Frequently Used Materials

For frequently used materials such as scissors, markers, and crayons, consider color coding them for use by small groups. For example, one group will always use the red set, and another group will always use the blue set. Since students will use the same set of materials day after day, they may take better care of them.

Plan Ahead When Using Materials

When materials are needed for a lesson, plan ahead by having student helpers organize the materials into bins or buckets. Then place a bin or bucket on each table.

Monitor Student Behavior

As students learn to use and return classroom items, observe carefully and narrate the behavior of students who properly place items where they belong.

Give Instructions Before Passing Out Materials

Give all preliminary instructions and answer any questions *before* you pass out materials. Students find it difficult to concentrate on new information when they have distracting materials in front of them. Establish a "hands off materials, stop, and listen" signal for any instructions or guidance you may need to give once materials are distributed.

Remind Helpers to Be Polite

If you use student helpers, remind them to be polite when they collect materials. If, for example, a student is still using an item, the helper should ask for the item politely and not grab it.

Make Sure Students Know How to Use Scissors

Most students know how to carry and use scissors safely, but it is still a good idea to review and demonstrate scissors safety. Review the safest way to hold scissors while walking (pointed end inside the palm) and to use scissors at a desk (set scissors down when they are not in use; do not wave them around).

Keep Classroom Library Organized

Establish a system to keep your classroom library organized as students check out and return books. One way to do this is to have students decorate and write their names on strips of poster board (approximately 4 x 12 inches each) that are then laminated for sturdiness. When students select a book from the classroom library, they leave their personalized strip as a marker. When returning a book, students find where it belongs on the shelf by locating their marker. Then they remove the marker and replace it with the book. This also helps you locate any books that are missing from the library. The personalized strips can be stored in a small box.

Chapter 45

Individual Students Leaving Class to Go to the Restroom

INTRODUCTION

There will be times when students will need to go to the restroom during class. If students must ask for permission, it tends to interrupt the instructional flow. A simple procedure can respect student needs and assure their prompt return with minimal disruption.

PLANNING

Determine Your Policy for Restroom Use During Class

Your policy may consider many factors, including student age and their level of responsibility.

- Most schools require students to carry a hall pass to identify their classroom and where they are going. Place the passes in a visible location near the door. Students need to be able to see if the pass is available or already in use.

- When students request to use the restroom, some teachers require students to first raise their hand. Upon being acknowledged by the teacher, the student points or nods in the direction of the hall pass. A nod back from the teacher lets the student know that it is okay to leave.

- Teachers of older students may allow them to leave class only for emergencies. Teachers of younger students sometimes use a buddy system and have two students go together to make sure they are safe and do not get sidetracked.

- Some teachers allow only one student, or one boy and one girl, to go to the restroom at a time.

PREVENTIVE MANAGEMENT STRATEGIES

Take Young Students to the Restroom

Make sure all students know where the restrooms are located. On the first day of school, you may want to take students on a quick tour to show them how to find the restroom.

Teach Young Students Appropriate Restroom Behavior

Teach students appropriate restroom manners. Discuss how to walk into the restroom, knock quietly to be sure a stall is empty, flush the toilet after use, wash hands, and throw away paper towels in the proper place.

Emergencies

Let students know that if they have a personal emergency and need to go to the bathroom very quickly, they can come up to you to let you know and then immediately leave.

Keep Track of Students Who Leave

To help track students who leave to use the restroom, make a vertical chart listing each student's name. Put two clothespins at the top of the chart—one marked "boys" and one marked "girls." If a student gets the nod to use the restroom, he or she clips the clothespin next to his or her name. You can tell at a glance who is gone from the room.

Be Alert

Be alert for special physical concerns that require a high frequency of restroom visits. Similarly, be aware of students who may take advantage of the policy.

Chapter 46

Late or Missing Assignments

INTRODUCTION

When students turn in assignments late or not at all, teachers too often handle situations on a case-by-case basis, which may result in favoring one student over another. This can cause problems with students and even their parents. To treat all students fairly, you need to determine the corrective actions that will apply if work is late and then apply these actions consistently. This will motivate students to complete their work in a responsible manner.

PLANNING

Determine Your Policy for Late or Missing Work

Some teachers are lenient and allow students to turn in assignments late without any penalty. Other teachers do not allow students to turn in any assignment past the due date. Most teachers find that the middle ground is the most useful starting point.

Consider these policy ideas:

- Any assignment turned in late receives a lower grade than it would have been given if turned in on time.

- Any assignment more than 1 week late will not be accepted.

- Contact the student's parents if more than three assignments are not turned in or are turned in late.

PREVENTIVE MANAGEMENT STRATEGIES

Send Policy Home to Parents

At the beginning of the year, send your policy regarding late or missing assignments home to parents. Ask them to sign and return it to school with their child.

Contact Parents at the First Sign of a Problem

Get in touch with parents as soon as it appears that a student is having trouble getting assignments in on time.

Introduce Homework Assignments in a Clear Manner

Be sure to introduce homework in a manner that is both clear and lets the students know the purpose of the assignment. Follow these guidelines:

- Always discuss the purpose of each assignment. For example: "Doing this homework will help you learn to write plural possessives correctly."

- Give clear, concise directions. When appropriate, give directions orally and in written form.

- Write homework assignments in the same place each day. Designate a portion of the board as the "homework corner," and keep the assignments up all week so students who are absent can readily determine their make-up work.

- Allow enough time for students to ask questions. Do not wait until the last minute to give the homework assignment, and do not assume that students understand what is required of them just because they have not asked any questions. To check understanding, ask students to tell you the directions in their own words.

- When appropriate, show examples of a successfully completed assignment. Model what is expected, or draw diagrams or pictures of what the final product should look like.

- When appropriate, allow students to begin the assignment in class. You can help answer questions as they arise, or ask students who understand the directions to model how they are doing the assignment.

Give Each Student a Planner

A planner will help students stay organized. Check to see if your school will provide commercial planners, or simply have each student use a spiral notebook. Students will write their daily assignments, long-term projects, and due dates in their planner and take it home each day. This allows them to keep track of their assignments and also helps keep their parents informed.

To help younger students learn organizational skills, provide each child with a blank monthly or weekly calendar. On your computer, type in each assignment and size it to fit inside a box on the calendar. Print multiple copies of the assignment. Then have students cut out each assignment and paste it into the appropriate box.

Use Positive Motivators

Positive motivators can help ensure students turn in their assignments on time.

Class homework chart:

- Place each student's name on a grid.

- When an assignment is returned on time, it earns a check or star.

- After a predetermined number of checks or stars, the student earns a privilege.

Positive notes to parents. Students of all grade levels appreciate notes to their parents recognizing the good work they are doing. Also, if parents are supporting you by checking to see that their children's assignments are turned in on time, they will appreciate knowing that their efforts are paying off. Be specific in your notes: "Michael has turned in all his assignments on time this week. You should be very proud."

Personal homework cards. This method of reinforcement allows individual students to earn points toward a reward each time a homework assignment is completed on time.

- Get a stack of index cards. With a pen or pencil, draw 10 or 20 boxes on each card (determine the number of boxes ahead of time). Or, create these boxes on computer and print the cards on heavy stock.

- Place a card on each student's desk.

- Each day that the student completes his or her homework, place a check or a sticker in one of the boxes.

- When the entire card is filled, the student earns a reward, such as extra free time or an award certificate.

Classwide homework raffle:

- This method gives all students who turn in assignments on time and appropriately done a chance to win a reward or prize.

- Tell students to write their names on both the left- and right-hand upper corners of their homework assignment papers.

- When their completed homework is turned in, tear off the right-hand corners of the papers and put them into a jar or box.

- At the end of the week, draw a name or two from the jar. The students whose names are drawn win extra free time, an opportunity to skip a homework assignment, or other raffle prizes.

Chapter 47

Student Helpers

INTRODUCTION

Student helpers, or monitors, can do a lot more for the classroom than make things easier for you. Being a student helper promotes responsibility and helps students feel ownership of the classroom and its contents.

PLANNING

As you plan for student helpers, determine:

- The jobs you want the student helpers to do

- The procedures for doing these jobs

- The method you will use to assign and track your classroom helpers

Decide the Jobs You Want to Assign to Student Helpers

The jobs you assign will be specific to your classroom needs. Keep in mind these guidelines:

- Doing the jobs should not impact a student's learning time.

- Jobs must be safe for the student to do.

- Jobs must be something that really needs to be done and enhances the classroom environment or helps get work done. Jobs should not be busywork.

- Jobs should be periodically rotated.

Student helpers can do many jobs, including the commonly assigned tasks listed on the next page.

Typical Student Helper Jobs

- Paper monitor
- Line leader
- Hall monitor
- Lunch helper
- Library helper/re-shelver
- Flag leader

- Computer support
- Homework collector
- Pencil monitor
- Calendar monitor
- P.E. equipment monitor

Determine How You Want Each Job to Be Done

You will need to teach your students how you expect each job to be done. Begin by writing down directions for doing each job. For example:

Calendar Monitor

At the beginning of class each day, the calendar monitor will change the date on the class calendar, check the weather on the Internet site, and update the day's weather on the board.

Pencil Monitor

At the end of class each day, the pencil monitor will sharpen all the dull pencils collected in the dull pencils can and place them in the sharp pencils can.

Develop a Student Helper Chart for Keeping Track of Monitors

Everyone in the class should be able to see at a glance who has what job at any given time. Here is a simple tracking idea:

- Make a chart with each student's name listed vertically down the left-hand side.
- Write each classroom job on a clothespin.
- Clip the job clothespin onto the student's name.
- Rotate jobs every week.

PREVENTIVE MANAGEMENT STRATEGIES

Teach Students How to Do Each Job

At the beginning of the year, model and teach each job so that every student can do each job. Make no assumptions—students may not know how to sharpen pencils or how to pass out papers the way you would like. Check for understanding and, if needed, periodically re-teach the jobs, especially if new students come into the classroom.

Fairly Assign Student Jobs

Some jobs will be more popular than others, and although you may appreciate student enthusiasm over being assigned these particular jobs, you do not want students to continually clamor for them.

Have a fair system for choosing student helpers. Drawing names is one method, or you can make choosing a job be an earned privilege. Keep a record of who has done what so all students have an opportunity to do as many jobs as possible.

Assign a Substitute Helper

Assign a student to be a substitute helper. If a classroom helper is absent or out of the room when his or her job needs to be completed, the substitute student can step in.

Use a Buddy System

Periodically allow a helper to select a friend to assist with his or her job. Working together will make the job more enjoyable and may even encourage students to complete the task in less time.

Involve Students in Determining Jobs

At the beginning of the year, ask students to brainstorm a list of jobs they might like to perform. You might not have thought of some of the jobs students will mention, and they will be motivated to carry out their suggestions.

Chapter 48

Taking Care of Desks, Tables, and Chairs

INTRODUCTION

Desks, tables, and chairs are important tools that are used constantly and must be kept in working order. Students need to be able to get materials from their desks quickly and quietly. They also need to be responsible for taking care of their desks, tables, and chairs.

PLANNING

Determine Your Policy for Care and Cleaning of Desks, Tables, and Chairs

Depending on the age of your students and your own classroom situation, you will want to develop specific expectations for how students are to care for their classroom equipment. Here are some ideas to consider:

- At the end of the day, all desktops (tabletops) are to be cleared of all materials.

- At the end of the week, clean out and either throw away or take home any loose papers that are not needed in class.

- The only things that should remain in desks are books, workbooks, and other classroom or school-related materials.

- Follow the rules of the school regarding what can and cannot be brought to school (toys, food, comic books, magazines, electronic games, phones, pagers).

- At the end of the day, all chairs are to be placed on top of tables.

- Once a week students are to wash off the tops of their desks and tables.

- Students should never look in another student's desk without permission.

- Students are not to draw or write on desks, tabletops, or chairs.

- Students are not to put stickers on desks, tabletops, or chairs.

PREVENTIVE MANAGEMENT STRATEGIES

Help Students Organize Desks

To transition smoothly between activities, students have to be able to locate their materials quickly and easily. Messy, disorganized desks can slow things down. Students who have the messiest desks tend to be those who have a habit of stuffing loose papers into the desk. Have students organize papers and supplies into folders and other containers. Decorating these folders or boxes can be a motivating activity as well as a practical endeavor. Here are some containers that can be decorated:

- Writing folders

- Math notebooks

- Literacy portfolios

- Pencil or pen cases

- Miscellaneous boxes (paper-clip boxes, eraser boxes, and so forth)

Clean Marked-Up Desks at an Appropriate Time

Teachers often have a rule that any student who draws on a desk or table must also clean it. That is fine, but do not have the student clean it during class time. Some students might regard this as a reward. Cleaning the desk during recess or after school is a more effective corrective action.

Establish Desk Clean-Up Time

Set a specific time at the end of each week for cleaning out desks. Keep an eye on younger students to make sure they do not throw away things that should be kept.

Display a List of Appropriate Desk Items

Create and display a list of appropriate desk items. Refer to the list when you teach students how to clean out their desks. For younger students, use pictures as a helpful reference. Keep this list on display and refer back to it periodically to remind students of your expectations.

Use "Kangaroo" Containers

"Kangaroo" containers are pouches attached to the back of students' chairs that can help students organize their clutter. Students can keep surplus materials such as markers, crayons, rulers, and protractors in this pouch. This will provide space inside the desk for essential items that are used daily. A simple pouch can be made from a pillow case or fabric remnant. Pouches can be personalized with fabric paint.

Chapter 49

Using the Drinking Fountain

INTRODUCTION

To avoid disruption of teaching and learning, students need to use the drinking fountain at specific times. Students also must use the fountain safely and with regard to the safety of others.

PLANNING

Determine Your Policy for Using Drinking Fountains

Your policy will depend on the age of your students, whether there is a fountain in your classroom, the distance of fountains from your classroom, time of year (weather), and responsibility level of your students.

Determine how students will use the fountain. Because using a drinking fountain means leaning over and getting teeth and mouth close to hard metal, students need to be taught to use fountains safely. Pushing or shoving at the drinking fountain could easily lead to injury. When using a fountain, students need to follow these directions:

- Line up single file and wait your turn.

- Do not touch another student in line or at the fountain.

- Do not spray or splash water at other students.

Determine when students will use the fountain. Your own policy will depend on where the fountains are located at your school: inside your classroom or on the yard. If both locations are available, decide when you expect students to use them.

On the yard. If the fountains are located on the yard or playground, students should be expected to take a drink before school and before they line up at the end of recess or lunch.

In the classroom. If fountains are located in the classroom and not on the yard or playground, let students line up and get drinks when they re-enter the classroom after recess and lunch. This means some students will be in line for a drink and others will go directly to their seats. Have both scenarios covered. Students waiting for a drink need to follow the rules (single file, no touching). Students not getting a drink need to follow your directions for re-entering the class and getting ready to work.

PREVENTIVE MANAGEMENT STRATEGIES

Teach Students How to Use Drinking Fountain (if Appropriate)

With younger students you may want to teach and demonstrate to students the appropriate and sanitary way to use a fountain:

- Carefully lean toward the fountain.

- Turn the water on.

- Drink from the stream of water. Do not touch the metal with your mouth.

Establish a Time Limit for Drinking

To keep the line at the drinking fountain moving, have a 10-second drinking limit (or 5 seconds, depending on what works best for you). Students must stop drinking when the other students finish counting to 10, for example.

Students Should Not Need Drinks During Instructional Time

If a sensible drinking fountain policy is in place, students should have ample opportunity to drink what they need before school, at recess, at lunch, during P.E., and after school. Unless the weather is unusually warm, teachers can reasonably expect older students to adhere to these times. Use your own judgment regarding whether students are abusing privileges by requesting extra water opportunities. In general it is best to be consistent in your expectations.

Let Students Bring Water Bottles

Some teachers allow students to bring water bottles to class, particularly during warm weather. They find this is less disruptive than excusing students to go to a fountain. Because keeping a water bottle at one's desk is a privilege, students are inclined to use them appropriately so the bottles will not be taken away. Be sure all bottles are marked with students' names in permanent marker and that students bring them home to wash them every day.

Appendix

Overhead Transparencies

Appendix

Overhead Transparencies

Paying Attention

✓ Keep your eyes on the teacher.

✓ Follow directions.

✓ Stay in your seat.

✓ Do not talk.

During a Class Discussion

✓ **Raise your hand and wait to be called on before speaking.**

✓ **Look at the student who is speaking.**

✓ **Stay seated.**

Classroom Management for Academic Success © 2006 by Solution Tree
www.solution-tree.com

Getting Ready to Go to the Rug

✓ **Stand up and quietly push in your chair.**

✓ **Stand behind your chair and wait to be told to come to the rug.**

✓ **Do not talk.**

Going to the Rug

✓ **Walk to the rug.**

✓ **Sit in your space.**

✓ **Keep hands and feet to yourself.**

✓ **Do not talk.**

Classroom Management for Academic Success © 2006 by Solution Tree
www.solution-tree.com

While on the Rug

✓ **Look at the teacher.**

✓ **Raise your hand and wait to be called on before speaking.**

✓ **Stay seated in your space.**

✓ **Follow directions.**

During Independent Work

✓ Stay in your seat.

✓ Do the assigned work.

✓ Do not talk.

✓ Use your Help Card.

✓ If you finish early, select an activity from the to-do list.

Classroom Management for Academic Success © 2006 by Solution Tree
www.solution-tree.com

Working With a Partner
Pairing Off

✓ Move quickly to sit with your partner.

✓ Speak in a quiet voice.

Working With a Partner

✓ Sit with your partner.

✓ Speak in a quiet voice.

✓ Work only on the assigned activity.

Moving Into a Small Group

✓ **Stand up quietly and push in your chair.**

✓ **Bring needed materials.**

✓ **Walk directly to the small group and take a seat.**

✓ **Do not talk.**

Working Independently at Your Seat

✓ **Do the assigned work.**

✓ **Save questions until we change groups (or use your Help Card).**

✓ **Stay seated.**

✓ **Do not talk.**

Classroom Management for Academic Success © 2006 by Solution Tree
www.solution-tree.com

Working With the Teacher in a Small Group

✓ **Follow directions.**

✓ **Raise your hand and wait to be called on before speaking.**

✓ **Stay seated.**

When Your Group Activity Is Finished

✓ Take your materials and go directly to your seat.

✓ Get right back to work.

✓ Do not talk.

When Working in a Group

✓ Work on the assignment.

✓ Stay seated.

✓ Talk only about the assignment and in a quiet voice.

Going to a Center

✓ **Stand up quietly and push in your chair.**

✓ **Bring the correct materials.**

✓ **Walk directly to the assigned center and take a seat.**

✓ **Speak in a quiet voice.**

When You Are at a Center

✓ Read the assignment first.

✓ Work on the assignment (by taking turns or as a group).

✓ Stay seated.

✓ Talk only about the assignment and in a quiet voice.

When Moving From One Center to Another

✓ Take your materials.

✓ Walk directly to the next center and sit down.

✓ Speak in a quiet voice.

At the Attention-Getting Signal

✓ **Freeze.**

✓ **Look at the teacher.**

✓ **Listen.**

In-Seat Transitions

When Ending One Activity and Getting Ready for Another

✓ Put away materials.

✓ Stay seated.

✓ Do not talk.

In-Seat Transitions
When Given Directions to Begin a New Activity

✓ Take out materials.

✓ Stay seated.

✓ Do not talk.

Out-of-Seat Transitions

Before Moving to a New Location to Begin a New Activity

✓ Follow the directions to complete the activity you are working on.

✓ Stay seated.

✓ Do not talk.

Classroom Management for Academic Success © 2006 by Solution Tree
www.solution-tree.com

Out-of-Seat Transitions

When You Are Ready for the Next Activity

✓ Stand up and quietly push in your chair.

✓ Wait for the signal to move.

✓ Do not talk.

Out-of-Seat Transitions

When You Are Told to Go

✓ **Follow directions.**

✓ **Walk directly to the next location.**

✓ **Remain quiet.**

Classroom Management for Academic Success © 2006 by Solution Tree
www.solution-tree.com

Lining Up

When You Are Told to Get Ready to Line Up

✓ Quietly push in chair and walk to the end of the line.

✓ Stand in a straight line without touching anyone.

✓ Wait to be dismissed from the classroom.

✓ Do not talk.

Walking in Line

When Given the "Go" Signal

✓ Walk directly behind the person in front of you.

✓ Keep your hands to yourself.

✓ Do not talk.

When Returning to Class After Recess or Lunch

✓ **Put away belongings and walk to your seat.**

✓ **Start the assignment on the board.**

✓ **Use your Help Card if you need the teacher's attention.**

✓ **Do not talk.**

Leaving the Classroom to Go to Another Program

✓ **Walk as you leave the classroom.**

✓ **Do not talk.**

✓ **Go directly to your assigned location.**

Returning From Another Program

✓ Walk into the classroom.

✓ Take your seat and get back to work.

✓ Do not talk.

When Distributing Papers

✓ Take just enough for yourself.

✓ Pass the rest to the next person in the row or at the table.

✓ Speak in a quiet voice.

When Collecting Papers

✓ **Place your paper on top of the other papers.**

✓ **Make sure your paper faces the same direction as the others.**

✓ **Speak in a quiet voice.**

www.solution-tree.com

275

When Attending an Assembly

✓ Sit in your seat.

✓ Do not talk.

✓ Clap or respond only when appropriate.

Classroom Management for Academic Success © 2006 by Solution Tree
www.solution-tree.com

When You Hear an Emergency Signal

✓ **Freeze.**

✓ **Stop talking.**

✓ **Follow directions.**

References

Arlin, M. (1979). Teacher transitions can disrupt time flow in classroom. *American Educational Research Journal, 16,* 42–56.

Armstrong, T. (1997). *The myth of the A.D.D. child: 50 ways to improve your child's behavior and attention span without drugs, labels or coercion.* New York: Plume.

Brophy, J. (1996). *Teaching problem students.* New York: Guilford.

Brophy, J. E., & Evertson, C. M. (1976). *Learning from teaching: A developmental perspective.* Boston, MA: Allyn and Bacon.

Canter, L., & Canter, M. (1976). *Assertive discipline: A take charge approach for today's educator* (1st ed.). Santa Monica, CA: Canter & Associates, Inc.

Canter, L., & Canter, M. (1992). *Assertive discipline: Positive behavior management for today's classroom* (2nd ed.). Santa Monica, CA: Canter & Associates, Inc.

Canter, L., & Canter, M. (1993). *Succeeding with difficult students: New strategies for reaching your most challenging students.* Santa Monica, CA: Canter & Associates, Inc.

Canter, L., & Canter, M. (2001a). *Assertive discipline: Positive behavior management for today's classroom* (3rd ed.). Santa Monica, CA: Canter & Associates, Inc.

Canter, L., & Canter, M. (2001b). *Parents on your side: A teacher's guide to creating positive relationships with parents* (2nd ed.). Los Angeles: Canter & Associates, Inc.

Canter, L., & Peterson, K. (1995). *Teaching students to get along.* Santa Monica, CA: Canter & Associates, Inc.

Charles, C. M. (1999). *Building classroom discipline* (6th ed.). New York: Longman.

Charles, C. M. (2000). *The synergetic classroom: Joyful teaching and gentle discipline.* New York: Longman.

Chui, L. H., & Tulley, M. (1997). Student preferences of teacher discipline styles. *Journal of Instructional Psychology, 24*(3), 169–175.

Cipriano Pepperl, J., & Lezotte, L. (2001). *High expectations.* Okemos, MI: Effective Schools Products.

Cotton, K. (1990). *School improvement series. Close-up #9: Schoolwide and classroom discipline.* Portland, OR: Northwest Regional Educational Laboratory.

Colvin, G., & Lazar, M. (1997). *The effective elementary classroom: Managing for success.* Longmont, CO: Sopris.

Curwin, R., & Mendler, A. (1999). *Discipline with dignity.* Alexandria, VA: Association of School Curriculum Development.

Emmer, E. T., & Hickman, J. (1991). Teacher efficacy in classroom management and discipline. *Educational and Psychological Measurement, 51,* 755–765.

Emmer, E. T., Sanford, J. P., Clements, B. S., & Martin, J. (1982). *Improving classroom management and organization in junior high schools: An experimental investigation.* Austin, TX: Research and Development Center for Teacher Education, University of Texas (R & D Report No. 6153). (ERIC Document Reproduction Service No. ED261053).

Emmer, E. T., Sanford, J. P., Evertson, C. M., Clements, B. S., & Martin, J. (1981). *The classroom management improvement study: An experiment in elementary school classrooms.* Austin, TX: Research and Development Center for Teacher Education, University of Texas (R & D Report No. 6050). (ERIC Document Reproduction Service No. ED226452).

Epstein, J. L., Clark, L., Salinas, K. C., & Sanders, M. G. (1997). Scaling up school-family-community connections in Baltimore: Effects on student achievement and attendance. Paper presented at the Annual Meeting of the American Educational Research Association. Chicago.

Evertson, C., & Harris, A. (1997). *COMP classroom organization and management program.* Nashville, TN: Vanderbilt University.

Gibs, N. (2005, February 21). Parents behaving badly. *Time, 165*(8), 40–49.

Good, T., & Brophy, J. (2003). *Looking in classrooms* (9th ed.). Boston, MA: Allyn and Bacon.

Gordon, D. T. (1999 September/October). *Rising to the discipline challenge.* Harvard Education Letter, 1–4.

Greenspan, S., & Salomon, J. (1996). *The challenging child: Understanding, raising and enjoying the five "difficult" types of children.* New York: Perseus Book Group.

Heim, P. (2001). Video program five: Engage all learners-presentation skills. In *Motivating today's learner,* pp. 41–47. Santa Monica, CA: Canter & Associates, Inc.

Henderson, A., & Mapp, K. (2002). *A new wave of evidence: The impact of school, family, and community connections on student achievement.* Austin, TX: Southwest Educational Development Laboratory.

Johnson, D., Maruyama, G., Johnson, R., Nelson, D., & Skon, L. (1981). Effects of cooperative, competitive, and individualistic goal structures on achievement: A meta-analysis. *Psychological Bulletin, 89*(1), 47–62.

Johnson, J. (2004, June 23). Why is school discipline considered a trivial issue? *Education Week, 23*(41), 48.

Jones, F. (2000). *Tools for teaching.* Santa Cruz, CA: Fred H. Jones & Associates, Inc.

Kerman, S., Kimball, T., & Martin, M. (1980). *Teacher expectations and student achievement.* Bloomington, IN: Phi Delta Kappan.

Kohn, A. (1993). *Punished by rewards.* Boston, MA: Houghton Mifflin.

Kounin, J. (1970). *Discipline and group management in classrooms.* New York: Holt, Rinehart and Winston, Inc.

LaFleur, L. H., Witt, J. C., Naquin, G., Harwell, V., & Gilbertson, D. (1998). Use of coaching to enhance proactive classroom management by improvement of student transitioning between classroom activities. *Effective School Practices, 17*(2), 70–82.

Langdon, C. (1996). The third Gallup/Phi Delta Kappa poll of teachers' attitudes toward the public schools. *Phi Delta Kappan, 78*(3), 244–250.

MacKenzie, R. (1996). *Setting limits in the classroom: How to move beyond the classroom dance of discipline.* Roseville, CA: Prima Publishing.

Marzano, R., Marzano, J., & Pickering, D. (2003). *Classroom management that works: Research-based strategies for every teacher.* Alexandria, VA: Association for Supervision and Curriculum Development.

Mendler, A. (2001). *Connecting with students.* Alexandria, VA: Association for Supervision and Curriculum Development.

Mendler, A., & Curwin, R. (1999). *Discipline with dignity for challenging youth.* Bloomington, IN: Solution Tree (formerly National Educational Service).

Metropolitan Life Insurance Co. (2005). *The MetLife survey of the American teacher 2004-2005.* New York: Metropolitan Life Insurance Company.

Public Agenda. (2004). Teaching interrupted: Do discipline policies in today's public schools foster the common good? Accessed October 19, 2005, from www.publicagenda.org

Riegler, H., & Baer, D. (1989). A developmental analysis of rule-following. *Advances in Child Development and Behavior, 21,* 191–219.

Rogers, S. (2001). *Teaching tips.* Evergreen, CO: Peak Learning Systems, Inc.

Rosenthal, R. (1974). *On the social psychology of the self-fulfilling prophecy: Further evidence for Pygmalion effects and their mediating mechanisms.* New York: MSS Modular Publications.

Rowe, M. (1986). Wait time: Slowing down may be a way of speeding up! *Journal of Teacher Education, 37,* 43–50.

Smith, R. (2004). *Conscious classroom management: Unlocking the secrets of great teaching.* San Rafael, CA: Conscious Teaching Publications.

Sprick, R., Garrison, M., & Howard, L. (1998). *CHAMPs: A proactive approach to classroom management.* Longmont, CO: Sopris West.

Stage, S. A., & Quiroz, D. R. (1997). A meta-analysis of interventions to decrease disruptive classroom behavior in public education settings. *School Psychology Review, 26*(3), 333–368.

Sugai, G., Horner, R., & Gresham, F. (2002). Behaviorally effective school environments. In M. Shinn, H. Walker, & G. Stoner (Eds.), *Interventions for academic and behavior problems II: Preventive and remedial approaches* (pp. 315–350). Bethesda, MD: National Association of School Psychologists.

Tauber, R. (1999). *Classroom management: Sound theory and effective practice.* Westport, CT: Bergin & Garvey.

Walker, H., & Walker, J. (1991). *Coping with noncompliance in the classroom: A positive approach for teachers.* Austin, TX: Pro-Ed.

Walker, H., Colvin, G., & Ramsey, E. (1995). *Antisocial behavior in school: Strategies and best practices.* Pacific Grove, CA: Brooks/Cole.

Walker, H., Ramsey, E., & Gresham, F. (2004). *Antisocial behavior in school: Evidence-based practices* (2nd ed.). Belmont, CA: Wadsworth/Thomson.

Wang, M. C., Haertel, G. D., & Walberg, H. J. (1993). Toward a knowledge base for school learning. *Review of Educational Research, 63*(3), 249–294.

Weinstein, R. S., & McKown, C. (1998). Expectancy effects in "context": Listening to the voices of students and teachers. In J. Brophy (Ed.), *Advances in research on teaching. Expectations in the classroom, 7,* 215–242. Greenwich, CT: JAI Press.

Whitaker, T. (2004). *What great teachers do differently.* Poughkeepsie, NY: Eye On Education.

Witt, J., LaFleur, L., Naquin, G., & Gilbertson, D. (1999). *Teaching effective classroom routines.* Longmont, CO: Sopris West.

Wong, K., & Wong, R. (1998). *First days of school: How to be an effective teacher.* Mountain View, CA: Harry K. Wong Publications.

Wright, S. P., Horn, S. P., & Sanders, W. L. (1997). Teacher and classroom context effects on student achievement: Implications for teacher evaluation. *Journal of Personnel Evaluation in Education, 11,* 57–67.

Make the Most of Your
Professional Development Investment

Let Solution Tree schedule time for you and your staff with leading practitioners in the areas of:

- **Professional Learning Communities** with Richard DuFour, Robert Eaker, Rebecca DuFour, and associates
- **Effective Schools** with associates of Larry Lezotte
- **Assessment *for* Learning** with Rick Stiggins and associates
- **Crisis Management and Response** with Cheri Lovre
- **Discipline With Dignity** with Richard Curwin and Allen Mendler
- **SMART School Teams** with Jan O'Neill and Anne Conzemius
- **PASSport to Success** (parental involvement) with Vickie Burt
- **Peacemakers** (violence prevention) with Jeremy Shapiro

Additional presentations are available in the following areas:

- Youth at Risk Issues
- Bullying Prevention/Teasing and Harassment
- Team Building and Collaborative Teams
- Data Collection and Analysis
- Embracing Diversity
- Literacy Development
- Motivating Techniques for Staff and Students

Solution Tree

555 North Morton Street
Bloomington, IN 47404
(812) 336-7700
(800) 733-6786 (toll-free number)
FAX (812) 336-7790
email: info@solution-tree.com
www.solution-tree.com

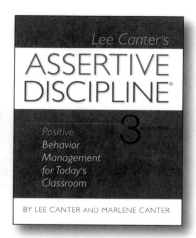
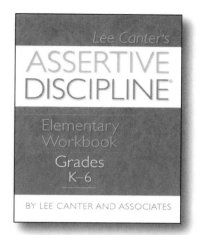
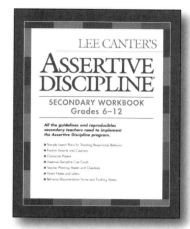

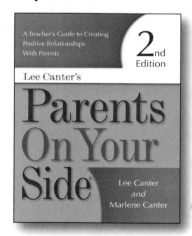